AMAZON ADS FOR INDIE AUTHORS

A HOW-TO GUIDE FROM AN INDUSTRY EXPERT

JANET MARGOT

Copyright © 2021 by Janet Margot

All rights reserved. No part of this book may be reproduced or used in any manner without written permission of the copyright owner except for the use of quotations in a book review. For more information, address: info@bookgeeksmarketing.com.

Book design by Micki Margot Design Studio

ISBNs:

    978-1-7374761-1-5 (paperback)

    978-1-7374761-0-8 (ebook)

www.bookgeeksmarketing.com

INTRODUCTION

It's pretty simple why you're here: You've published your book through Kindle Direct Publishing (KDP), and it's now listed in Amazon marketplaces globally. Amazon has the largest customer base, and you want to tap into its readers browsing onsite. You may get some sales here and there, but can you sell more? Welcome to the world of Amazon Ads.

I'm writing this book to share the knowledge I gained from a decade at Amazon working on their ads platform. I joined Amazon Ads when it was a tiny program for third-party sellers only, an inconceivable universe where we actually drove customers *off* Amazon! Clearly that was not a popular program throughout Amazon retail ranks, and Amazon Marketing Services (AMS), now known as Sponsored Ads, was borne (killing off the original ad program).

Given my previous life in publishing and vocal love of books, I was handpicked by senior leadership to help build out the new book ads team in 2015. I was Head of Marketing, Account Management and Operations before transitioning to a Product Manager role in hopes that I could more directly influence features for books. I left book ads in December of 2019, moving over to work on video ad technology in another part of the company.

During that time, I worked closely with engineers, product managers, and marketers who were charged with supporting book ads. I had conversations with countless authors listening to their pain points and delivered some of their top asks. I analyzed huge amounts of data. This insider experience sets me apart from other ad 'experts' out there. Since leaving Amazon, I've been working one-to-one with authors, putting my knowledge to the test. I've modified some of the best practices and learned a lot along the way. I also teach Amazon Ads to authors enrolled in Mark Dawson's Self Publishing Formula classes.

My goal is for this book to cut through the noise of advice that's out there and deliver the most authoritative information available on how Amazon Ads work for books. I won't be shy when I don't know something: I'll offer you an educated hypothesis based on what I do know. I won't pretend something's fact when it's a personal observation. I won't give you gimmicks. I won't make up names for things because they're cute; instead, I'll stick with industry standards. Lastly, I will help you to understand which ad features should be questioned when implementing them for books and why.

This book takes a cautious and simple approach to ads that drives growth efficiently. This requires patience on your part, as I am not here to help you go from 0 to 60 quickly. That approach doesn't work and, if it did in the short term, I bet it wouldn't last (in fact, I'll tell you why).

My mission is for indie authors to eventually be able to spend less time with ads, and more time creating the books we all love to read.

IMPORTANT NOTE! Amazon frequently updates its ads platform. Information in this book is accurate at time of writing but can quickly change. Before you start reading, sign up for updates to this book at: **www.bookgeeksmarketing.com/amazon-ad-book-news-and-updates**.

BEGINNER ONLY: GETTING STARTED FOR FIRST TIMERS

If you have experience advertising, skip ahead to Part One.

This is ground zero. This chapter is for you if you are totally new to ads or a first timer with ads on Amazon. Either way, if you're nervous about creating ads, you're not alone. The advertising world is rife with lingo and technical terms, which can be daunting. You do not need to know everything from the start.

By the end of this section, you will be off, running, and able to run your first basic ads. I will walk you through the steps to get you launched with your very first campaigns. Together we will keep it simple while you build knowledge.

You will learn how to create a Sponsored Products automatic campaign where Amazon does the heavy lifting for you. These ads will need to run a week or two before we can take further action. While these ads are running, you will be collecting some feedback on the ad while you continue to learn more by reading on.

You need two things on hand to get started: your kdp.amazon.com login and your credit card (to pay for ads).

Creating Your First Ads Account

If you do not yet have an ads account, you'll need to create one. Start in your KDP portal.

- Click on "Marketing" in the top navigation bar.
- Halfway down the page you'll see "Advertising."
- Select the country where you'd like to start advertising.

Once you select a country, you'll be automatically ported into the registration pipeline for ads.

You'll be prompted to enter your KDP credentials (which will now also be your ads credentials) and credit card details for payment.

Recommendation: If your book is written in English, start in the US, where the largest customer base is. This will mean that your ads will garner the largest amount of data and you'll learn faster. When you're ready to start advertising in an additional country, this is where you will return to start the process again.

Creating Your First Campaign

When you're in the ads console for the first time, you will be prompted to choose a campaign type. Select Sponsored Products, because it is the most consistently performing type of self-service ads, the easiest to get started with, and the most fully baked for the Books category.

Clicking "continue" drops you into the Sponsored Products campaign builder. If you haven't already entered your credit card details, you may see an alert at the top to add a payment method in order to be able to launch your campaign.

Input your settings

1. *Fill in a campaign name.* Create a campaign name overriding the default. The naming convention should be descriptive so that you can identify the nature of your campaign when you first visit your top-level dashboard. My go-to campaign naming convention is [book name]+[ad type]+targeting+[date]. Using this book as an example, the campaign name would be "AA+SP+Auto+July21."
2. *Set start and end dates.* The default start date is the current date, but you can set a date to start running the ad in the future. You can keep the end date set to none or choose your own end date. For your first campaign, make sure it is no less than one month out, but I prefer not to set an end date.
3. *Set a daily budget.* I recommend starting with a daily budget of $10 a day. Anything less will make it difficult to capture the volume of data that we need to get by running our first campaign.
4. *Choose targeting type.* Select automatic targeting. Amazon will look at the data surrounding your book, select keywords and products that are similar to your book and target the ad against those.
5. *Select campaign bidding strategy.* Select fixed bids. These are known to drive a higher volume of impressions, which is what we are after in our first ad(s). I cover the different bidding strategies in full in Chapter 8. You can ignore the adjustments by placement at this point. Double check that the percentages in each of those boxes equals zero.

6. *Select ad format.* Click the radio button to select Standard Ad, which is best for beginners. While Amazon defaults to the "Custom Text" option for KDP authors, your first campaign should be about learning ad mechanics, and the custom text option will only muddy the waters. This means that the ad creative will only include elements already in the catalog: the book cover, the title, the price, and star ratings.
7. *(Don't) Name your ad group.* Even though we are only creating one ad group for this campaign, Amazon is creating an ad group on your behalf. There is no need to name it.
8. *Select products to advertise.* In the left column of this box, you should see a list of your books published through KDP, including both digital and print formats. Select one book that you want to advertise and click "add." That book should now have moved to the right column in the box.
9. *Set bids.* Under automatic targeting, select "default bid." Choose an amount that you are comfortable with. This should be the highest price that you are willing to pay for a click on your ad. Of course, we are hoping Amazon is smart enough to provide good targets for the first auto campaign, but we cannot be confident. As a new advertiser, your risk tolerance should not be overly aggressive. You are here to learn and to do so, you need data. Bid high enough to gain insight into what works. I suggest $.50 is a good starting point.
10. *Negative targeting.* Leave negative targeting blank. Any term or product assigned here will be excluded from your ads targeting. Negative targeting use cases covered more in Chapter 5. Once you have run ads for a while, this feature is invaluable for driving precision and spend efficiency.

At this point you should be ready to scroll to the bottom of the screen and hit the orange "launch campaign" button. Voila! Your ad will now be moderated by the ads team, and you should receive an email that provides a status update within 24 hours.

Next Steps for First Timers

Allow your new ad to simmer while you learn the finer points of Amazon advertising as outlined in this book. Your ad will need to run for at least one week before we peek at any data, and should run for a full two weeks before we make changes. This is because the dashboard reports on sales and pages read that occur within 14 days of the click. Acting on an ad prematurely can block a campaign from reaching its potential.

PART I
AMAZON

We often refer to Amazon as if it's a single entity. In fact, it's a convergence of many factions of business to form a customer experience. As an author, understanding where you sit in the mix of advertising, retail and subscriptions helps shed light on where it makes sense to insert yourself on the purchase path of potential readers.

CHAPTER 1
IMPORTANCE OF RETAIL

Amazon has over 300 million active customer accounts worldwide and has officially surpassed Walmart as the largest retail seller outside of China. In 2020, the site had had 213 million unique visitors per month in the US alone, capturing 41 cents of every dollar spent online in the US.[1]

Prime membership grew to 200 million members globally in 2020 and to 147 million in the US alone in 2021.[2] These Prime customers are loyal and are already in the mindset to purchase.

Their customer base is so desirable in both quantity and quality that even industries who can't sell directly on Amazon run big budget ad campaigns. For example, you may see ads for credit cards although financial services companies cannot list their services in the marketplace. These banks can only run big-budget ads with giant placements but they are not eligible for self-service advertising.

There are three main types of business working with Amazon who have access to self-service ads: Vendors, Sellers and KDP Authors. The topic of who can do what comes up often, so I will offer a brief description.

Vendors – Definition and Backstory

Vendors are entities that have a true retail relationship with Amazon. This is the classic way that a manufacturer or brand will sell to retailers like Barnes & Noble, Waterstones, Walmart or Tesco. In the old-school brick-and-mortar days, many of these retail agreements required vendors to commit to spending a percentage of their forecasted sales on what they called "co-op": additional promotional opportunities like funding mailers with coupons or in-store displays such as the "end cap" displays anchoring prominent aisles or front-of-store tables.

In the books category today, these vendors are traditional publishing houses, their imprints, mid-list publishers, textbook/academic presses and classic distributors of all sizes. These book vendors print their own books and negotiate with Amazon to "sell in" a certain sales volume.

Distributors may handle selling into the trade (online and physical bookstores) on behalf of publishers and presses of all sizes. This distributor designation can include print-on-demand (POD) services like IngramSpark, even though the sell-in volume for POD is not negotiated. Instead, the POD catalog is just piped into Amazon catalog.

Vendors use a portal called Vendor Central to list, price and manage their products on Amazon. This is their portal to create an ads account as well.

There is a subset of vendors called "Advantage" vendors who produce or sell physical media goods (books, DVDs, CDs). They do not sell their products outright to Amazon; instead, they sell them on consignment. This entity type uses Advantage Central to create and manage listings and to access advertising. This vendor type does not support digital products. Both types of vendors have the same console.

Sellers – Definition and Backstory

The largest population of entities with products flowing through Amazon is third-party sellers. They are also the biggest population of advertisers. Sellers do not have a negotiated retail relationship as the vendors do. Sure, it's a relationship subjected to terms and conditions, but they do not negotiate an up-front sell-in; in other words, Amazon does not buy the products directly. Instead, they contract to use Amazon's third-party marketplace platform to sell to customers. They can fulfill orders themselves directly or use Fulfillment by Amazon (FBA).

Sellers list and manage their products using Seller Central, which is Amazon's most robust retail tool. This is their gateway to advertising.

KDP Authors – Definition and Backstory

Kindle Direct Publishing (KDP) authors have the most interesting retail relationships with Amazon because the heart of the relationship is not just a selling platform, it's an actual content publishing platform that drives access to Amazon's customers in its stores worldwide.

KDP authors use kdp.amazon.com as their portal for listing and managing titles; this is also their gateway to Amazon Ads registration. Once registered for advertising initially, they can manage ads through advertising.amazon.com. Advertising for KDP authors is available in the United States, United Kingdom, Germany, France, Italy, Spain, Australia and Canada.

---

1. NYTimes, 8/17/2021 Shoppers buy $600 billion dollars' worth of products on Amazon each year.
2. Statista, July 5, 2021.

CHAPTER 2
ADVERTISING ON AMAZON

As an author, you can not only directly point prospective customers to your book, but the ad platform offers the ability to specifically target *high-probability* book buyers. This book only tackles how self-service advertising works for Kindle Direct Publishing (KDP) authors.

Why Advertise on Amazon

If you're wondering why you should invest in paid advertising on Amazon, the answer is indisputable: the customers are there. Amazon was founded on bookselling, so it's no surprise that books/music/video is one of two verticals where Amazon receives the majority (83.2%) of US ecommerce sales in 2021. (Computer/consumer electronics is the second at 50.2%.)[1] All sellers in all categories are out for product discovery, but you can imagine how amplified the need for visibility is in these verticals. The sheer number of books released annually makes discoverability the key hurdle when listing books on Amazon. 30% of global surveyed book buyers visit Amazon to research a book, even if they don't end up purchasing from Amazon.[2]

Amazon's investments in books went far beyond retail with the launch of the Kindle Direct eBook publishing platform in 2007, followed by subscription programs like the Kindle Lending Library (2011), Kindle Unlimited (2014), and Prime Reading (2016). Subscriptions are increasingly popular, with over 3 million readers subscribed to Kindle Unlimited (pre-COVID)[3]. Amazon continues to make reading more available to more users, even launching a program (Kindle Vella) for fans of episodic fiction in 2021.

These programs make it easier for Amazon to keep customers within the Amazon universe and for customers to further engage with more books. According to Bowker, which sells ISBNs to publishers, Amazon publishes 92% of all self-published books from hundreds of thousands of indie authors. With the abundance of titles, authors and publishers turn to paid advertising to boost title visibility.

The number one way readers get turned on to a new book is to have it recommended by someone they know. In the digital space, that means building mechanisms online to mimic valuable human recommendation. Amazon created an advertising universe where book ads have become akin to a recommendation engine driving title discovery.

The Ads Ecosystem

Amazon Ads is a large portfolio of ad products made available to authors and publishers of all sorts, from billion-dollar companies to little mom-and pop-businesses, with author-entrepreneurs (that's you, KDP Authors) falling somewhere in-between.

Within the Amazon Ads umbrella, there are two main channels of advertising: display ads (formerly known as AMG or Amazon Marketing Group), which is a managed premium service, and Sponsored Ads (formerly known as AMS or Amazon Marketing

Services), which is self-service. Display ads require a large minimum spend. For that spend, you'll get an account manager and guaranteed impressions. Instead of relying on the catalog book cover only, managed display ads offer the ability to run ads with your custom ad creative. Your dedicated campaign manager sets up the campaigns and targeting designed to hit that impression guarantee that you're buying. You don't have direct access to hands-on reporting, and you won't be in control of optimizing your ads.

Only a small subset of authors can afford to go big, sounding all the bells and whistles. For the rest of us, Amazon offers accessible and cost-effective self-service ads called Sponsored Ads. This program is available to all KDP authors.

Why Use Sponsored Ads?

The competition out there is stiff, making organic discovery near impossible for most authors. This is nothing new. Book discovery has been a challenge for years before we had KDP and before the internet became our best friend. If you want to sell books as a valid source of income, you need to learn how to market them. That can mean a lot of different things. Social media posts, promos, email blasts, and word of mouth can all lend a hand in promoting your book and attracting buyers to your listing, but a strategic advertising campaign is a great way to zero in on readers and increase sales.

Using Sponsored Ads allows you to directly compete with traditional publishers for reader's attention. This is a big plus for indies who, lacking the support of a marketing team that a traditionally published author may have, are effectively blocked from some marketing channels. Despite various conspiracy theories about how Amazon gives publishers preferential treatment, the only people who have a leg-up with Sponsored Ads are those who implement them well.

Sponsored Ads are considered "performance ads" because you pay for performance, rather than to display. Payment is a standard pay-per-click (PPC) or cost-per-click (CPC) business model. This means that you get impressions for free and only pay when shoppers click on your ad, saving your ad budget for those who express a further interest in your book. PPC is inexpensive compared to display advertising and the minimum spend is negligible – but there are no promises of success on a dollar-a-day budget!

These ads are completely self-service. There is no application required and no need to work with an Amazon employee to get started. Impressions are not guaranteed. The ad creative is based on the book cover, with ad types offering some limited options to customize certain ad elements.

The PPC ad model is auction-based, such that you bid against other authors to show your ad to browsers based on specified criteria. In short, you're telling Amazon "I want to show my ad to people who are searching for X and I'm willing to pay $$Y$ to do it."

---

1. eMarketer, Amazon dominates US ecommerce, though its market share varies by category, Apr 27, 2021
2. Amazon and Kantar books path to purchase study, March 2021, advertising.amazon.com
3. Forbes, January 2020 https://www.forbes.com/sites/billrosenblatt/2020/01/03/why-ebook-subscription-services-will-finally-succeed-in-the-coming-decade

CHAPTER 3
THE AD TYPES

KDP authors have access to three types of ads as of this writing: Sponsored Products, Sponsored Brands and Lockscreen Ads. Understanding the ad types helps you work out how to bring your catalog closer to the right reader during their customer journey. Think about how to combine all multiple ad types to enable various touchpoints during the shopping experience to capturing a customer's click.

Sponsored Products

What are they? All authors should focus their time on Sponsored Products, regardless of where you are in your author or book lifecycle. These ads are designed to deliver measurable results: to increase search visibility and boost sales. Sponsored Product ads appear in search results, sometimes in multiple places, including the top, middle and bottom. They also appear in a carousel on every detail page of the Amazon catalog. These are the most consistent and the standard placements (although they may temporarily power other placements from time to time). Keyword, product, or category targeting options are available. The basic ad type has no creative options other than book cover (and price), but book advertisers have the option to use a decoration called "custom text" (US only). Although you can include multiple books in an ad campaign, only one individual book will display at a time. When a customer clicks on the ad, they are brought to the detail page that includes the book description and the buy button.

Sponsored Products are considered Amazon's flagship ad product and has been its longest running. This is the most consistent ad product and has had the highest investment by Amazon for book ads. They work well for both backlist and new releases, as readers often view them as "recommendations" even though they are sponsored.

Why use them? With studies showing that 70% of Amazon users don't make it past the first page of search results,[1] Sponsored Products can help boost your visibility. They are the easiest ads to get running. The content featured in the ad, including the imagery, is straight from the Amazon catalog. When you are just learning, you can employ automatic targeting to have Amazon do all the work.

Recommendation: Sponsored Products should be at the core of any ads strategy. Experiment with different targeting options for your books. See Chapter 5 All About Targeting.

Lockscreen Ads

What are they? Lockscreen ads are full screen ads that appear primarily on the home screen and lock screen of Kindles. This is a single-title creative that includes a teaser along with the book title. Creative varies slightly between e-reader and Fire tablets. The ad creative includes your book cover, your star reviews and a custom text (or "blurb") that serves as a teaser. When the ad is clicked, it sends the shopper to your eBook detail page. If the device is not connected to the internet, the shopper may need to go to an interstitial page. These ads spotlight a single book at a time and reach readers on Amazon devices, so only eBooks are eligible. Lockscreen Ads are exclusive to KDP authors and publishers but there is a premium version of the placement available through the managed display team.

Why use them? You can easily target readers by the genre purported in their reading experience if Kindle is the device they are likely to use. With 67% of e-reader owners being female, these can be strong for female-centric genres like romance or even thrillers with female protagonist.[2] Given the digital nature, they are great for genres with a high volume of customers in Kindle Unlimited.

Recommendation: Use Lockscreen Ads for a 1–3 month flight to push a big new release or a high-volume backlist seller. In October to December, the inventory is sold to priority advertisers, so it's only worth including Lockscreen Ads on your plan outside of these times. Know that this is icing on your ads cake; because there is a high risk of the ad not taking flight (not starting due to lack of available impressions), you can't count on this for the guts of a strategy.

Sponsored Brands

What are they? Previously called Headline Search, Sponsored Brands appear prominently above-the-fold and above search results before all other ad types. Recently this ad type expanded to secondary placement in middle of search "other" placements. Sponsored Brands are well-suited to advanced advertisers and advantageous for those with larger catalogs. Three books, along with a custom headline and author headshot or logo, appear in this horizontal ad slot. When a customer clicks, they land on a custom landing page, curated by you, with multiple titles for readers to browse. Targeting options are manual, with keyword, product and category targeting available. This is considered a longer ad play in which brand-building gains may not come so quickly. There are more clicks required to get to the "buy" button, often meaning the ad may appear more expensive than Sponsored Products.

Why use them? This ad slot is valuable for your brand-building. Sponsored Brands work well for a series or collection of related titles or themes. The custom landing page allows readers to engage with a larger swath of your catalog (that you define). There is significant value to being the first slot for an important query but this may come at a higher cost than other ad types.

Recommendation: Try Sponsored Brands only once you have confidence in your target market as validated via Sponsored Products campaigns. Consider using this ad type to reinforce repeat purchases by customers with the highest purchase intent. Do this by running against your own brand terms. (See Chapter 20 for more on Brand Defense),

Sponsored Brands may be more costly than Sponsored Products and are not the best "always-on" campaign; instead, use this strategically for short periods of time. Closely monitor newly launched campaigns to mitigate runaway spend.

---

1. Search Engine Journal. Amazon's Search Engine Rankings Algorithm. https://www.searchenginejournal.com/amazon-search-engine-ranking-algorithm-explained/265173/#close
2. This is not to say that only women read stories with female protagonists.

CHAPTER 4
TITLE ELIGIBILITY AND GUIDELINES

If you are new to Amazon Ads or are entering a new genre, take 15 minutes to confirm that your book is eligible for advertising. Guidelines for publishing using KDP do not cover advertising; advertising has its own guidelines. Just because you can list it and sell it, does not mean that you can advertise it. Your title, cover and content should meet the requirements set forth in the Book Ads Guidelines and Acceptance Policies (the Guidelines)[1].

Authors are limited to promoting titles that are already being sold on Amazon via your KDP account. You cannot use Amazon Ads to advertise titles printed via other, non-Amazon print-on-demand (POD) services. Your book must be available for sale in whichever locale you're trying to advertise. For example, if you're trying to advertise in Italy, your book must be available for sale on Amazon.it.

There are some genres that are particularly sensitive: Romance, Mystery Thriller Suspense and Self Help Books. Again, this is regardless of whether they are ok to sell. Controversial imagery may include: anything sexually suggestive, excessive skin, positioning of weapons, amount of blood or gore, use of alcohol, tobacco, drugs, or drug paraphernalia, minors.

Enforcement of the guidelines varies slightly by country. These rules are written generally enough to apply worldwide, although the policy's application may change slightly by marketplace. Even between countries like the US and the UK, there are vast differences in how the public perceives things like nudity or violence. Other countries may have more sensitivity around politics or religion. These differences will be evaluated by Amazon moderators. The major content exclusion applied uniformly worldwide is erotica. Erotic books are not eligible for advertising.

Ad Approval Process

Book ads go through review before they can go live in any Amazon marketplace via a process called "moderation." Whenever you create an ad, the book cover, title, content, and any custom elements are reviewed. The process begins while you are creating your ad. Sometimes you'll notice "inline moderation" as the campaign builder highlights basic areas to fix and will block you from finalizing the campaign if you have spelling, grammar or restricted character errors.

After your ad is submitted, you should get an email stating that you've submitted the ad and it's in internal review. This may take up to 72 hours, but typically they turn around decisions within 24 hours – often even less.

This means that your ad has been moved on to be seen by a moderator. Yes, Amazon has humans reviewing book ads. Moderators are looking to ensure that your ad may be seen by a general audience without doing harm. What you consider appropriate for a certain audience may not apply to customers at large, particularly as families share devices and customer accounts. They will flag content that violates this general suitability.

You will receive an email from Amazon to let you know whether your ad was approved or not. If your ad was rejected, the email should include a reason for this.

Recommendation: Save yourself frustration by making sure that, to the best of your knowledge, the cover and the content of the book are following the guidelines. (Guidelines.)

---

1. Book Ads Guidelines and Acceptance Policies, https://advertising.amazon.com/en-us/resources/ad-policy/book-ads

PART II
HOW ADS WORK

This is my kindergarten version of how ads work. An engineer would cringe to read this!

Your bundle of book+ bid + targeting is an ad. Your "book" also includes its retail metadata. When you create an ad campaign, all elements are reviewed by a moderation team. Once approved, the bundle is then sent to a "holding bin." It's here where your relevance is assessed. When a customer searches for or browses books, there will be an opportunity for an ad to show for that target. The algorithm collects all the ads that have relevant targeting and pulls them together into an auction. This bundle of [book+ bid + targeting] + relevance competes against your peers who are also trying to win that reader's attention. The ad with the combination of highest bid and highest relevance should win the auction. You are assigned a price for that click based on the auction outcome (cost-per-click or CPC); these CPCs are only charged if the customer clicks.

Note that there is not a sole winner; many ads "win" because there are usually multiple placement opportunities (for example, the ads carousel on the detail page). In that case, they are ranked and displayed accordingly.

When a customer clicks on the ad and then buys the advertised book, this conversion (sale or pages read) is recorded (or attributed) to that click.

This gross over-simplification should provide insight into how some of the following key concepts are applied.

CHAPTER 5
ALL ABOUT TARGETING

Targeting is the mechanism that connects your book with a reader. For example, let's say that I am advertising a regency romance and want to target readers who search for the author Julia Quinn because she is successful in that sub-genre. I'll need to encourage Amazon to show my book at the right time to the right people, who I believe to be Julia Quinn's readers.

Amazon offers various targeting tactics that can be used in conjunction with one another to touch readers throughout their browsing journey. You may hear authors talk authoritatively about what targeting works and what does not, but it is rare that one way works well for everyone. Each book – even in the same genre or even from the same author – will have a distinct set of variables impacting performance. You'll need to experiment across targeting tactics.

Automatic vs Manual Targeting

At a high level, there are two branches of targeting: automatic and manual.

Automatic Targeting

In automatic ads, Amazon chooses the keywords and products similar to the advertised book, based on your metadata. This allows you to create a campaign easily and quickly. Amazon applies four matching strategies (also called targeting groups): Close match, Loose Match, Substitutes, and Complements. You have the option to bid differently by each strategy. For example, you may want to bid higher for a close match because it is expected to be of higher value to you.

Manual Targeting

Manual campaigns put you in control. There are three types of manual targeting options: keyword, product, and category. Within each, Amazon will offer suggested targets, but you can also use a list you create yourself. While this requires more work, it gives you a greater precision in choosing targets.

Recommendation:

(1) Use automatic targeting if you are a new advertiser or on any book that you are advertising for the first time. This allows you to see what connections are being made between your book and others in the catalog. Start with a single bid across targeting groups. Once your campaign is live, monitor which targeting groups are getting impressions and sales. You can then make your decisions based on each group's performance and adjust the bids by targeting group accordingly.

(2) Use manual when you are ready to take control. Start with Amazon's suggestions while you research and craft a list based on what you know about your readers.

Keyword Targeting

A keyword is a word or phrase that describes your book and enables readers to find your book. Keywords are a targeting mechanism – the keywords you choose determine when and where your ad appears and to which customers. You want to get it as close to a customer search term as possible. It may be an actual book title or author name. If non-fiction, perhaps its topical.

Keyword targeting allows you to choose relevant terms to match your book to readers. These may be individual words or phrases. Keyword targeting is available within both Sponsored Products and Sponsored Brands.

Tip: An ASIN or ISBN cannot be used as a keyword. Although you can technically include the ASIN as a keyword target and the dashboard will accept it, the keyword ad will not actually serve against an ASIN target.

There are three different match types allowing you to fine tune how you want to connect to shoppers' search queries: broad, phrase and exact. These reflect the perceived level of purchase intent.

Broad match: This offers your ad broad traffic exposure. Your term, which can be a string of words, will match if the customer's query includes all those words in any order. It may include synonyms and plurals. But the match does not stop there, and this is where it can get expensive as it becomes potentially over-reaching: the phrase may also match to "related" shopping queries or "close variations." I find this to be too wildly ambiguous for serious investment. I use broad match when I want to cast a wide net, with the intent of finding which customer search terms will convert to sales. I then switch from broad match to other match types for that customer search term.

Phrase match: The search term must contain the exact phrase or sequence of words. This also includes plurals. Customer search terms matching to phrase match have a better idea of what they want; they have stronger purchase intent than broad matches.

Exact match: The search term must exactly match the keyword or sequence of words for the ad to show. It will also match to slight variations and plurals. Exact match will be restrictive in terms of reach but is often one of the best mechanisms to use on a proven target. In my experience, this has been the best match type when targeting strong comp author names as there is the highest purchase intent. For other names, that may be a weaker connection, phrase can work better.

Recommendation: Start your initial manual keyword campaigns using the following types of strings: author names, genre tropes, author titles. Note that I do not recommend very general terms like "book." The ad you make using auto targeting will generate enough of those connections, and you can see if they work there. Using a very general term in your manual campaign is unlikely to pay off consistently in sales or royalties in the long run.

Start by experimenting with all three match types.

Allow your campaign to run for two weeks and review the data. Then narrow down which match type(s) work best for your ad.

Product & Category Targeting

Product targeting is a little confusing in the ads dashboard. It's named "product" targeting, but when you drill down, you have two options: product or category targeting. Internally, Amazon teams refers to this as "product *attribute* targeting" (aka PAT) because it allows an advertiser to refine targeting towards specific product attributes: brand, price range, review star ratings, and Prime shipping eligibility. Not all of these are valuable for book advertisers. Brand does not include author name, so it's not possible to target an author's catalog using this feature. Because of the overuse of the word 'product,' I'll refer to this tactic as "ASIN targeting" vs category targeting.

Product Targeting a/k/a ASIN targeting

This allows you to specify which detail pages you want your ad to show on. For example, if I am a new Romantic Suspense author, I may think about capturing readers of a popular series like Barbara Freethy's *Off the Grid* FBI series. My hope is that readers browsing her detail pages would see my book cover, find my title interesting, and add my book to their cart. In that case, I would make a list of all the ASINs in the *Off the Grid* series and import them into an ASIN targeted campaign.

Alternatively, Amazon will suggest products they consider to be like your advertised ASIN. These ASIN suggestions are hit or miss. Luckily suggestions include the title, star rating, price, and cover, so you can easily scan for only those titles appearing relevant.

ASIN targeting can be costly but it should be the most precise targeting. However, it appears that some of these ads may be surfacing in other slots beyond the targeted ASIN detail page. Authors report mixed feedback about these ads: they either do not take off or they are expensive but do convert.

Recommendation: Create two ad groups when starting with ASIN advertising. The first group should be Amazon's suggested ASINs and the second should be a list that you create.

Category targeting

This allows you to designate the genres in which you would like your ad to show. The ad will show on book detail pages in that category. Once again, Amazon will provide suggestions that can be questionable. Sometimes these are your actual categories and sometimes they are determined from elsewhere. For example, if I'm advertising a Sci-Fi & Fantasy title, it may suggest Horror Literature, where my book is not classified because "horror" does not describe my book. As with ASIN targeting, review these suggestions carefully to avoid spending on irrelevant clicks.

The ad builder here can be insightful in that it displays the intended reach. For example, if I choose a subcategory of Fairy Tale Fantasy, it shares that there are 1153–1921 products that may be targeted. This is a narrow reach, but, if this is highly relevant to the advertised book, then it is expected to be a valuable target.

However, if I select Fairy Tale Fantasy and click on "Refine," there is a brand (rather than a genre) drop-down. This brand functionality is not enabled. These refinements can be a mixed bag of helpfulness but valuable when Amazon has the feature enabled. Do not overlook this option!

If you are not satisfied with Amazon's suggestions, you can search categories and still make refinements, when meaningful drop-downs are available. As of this writing, the ad builder only lists the Books category, not the Kindle eBooks category. The two browse trees are different. Under Books, the breadth of subgenres will differ by genre. For some genres, you may find that there are an extremely limited number of subgenres available, whereas for others it is built out more robustly. For some genres, this may not seem like a solid feature, but for others there are strong options available for further refinements. For example, if I select Sci Fi & Fantasy, I have three subgenre refinements available to choose from. However, if I select Fantasy Gaming, it allows me to then refine to a list of nearly 20 options that are highly specific.

When working with category ads, if you do not use refinements, your ad is likely to be blasted broadly. This is how category ads get expensive. The book categories and subcategories are well-known to be very "polluted" by misclassification so your blast can become a misfire. For example, at time of writing there is a Romantic Suspense title ranking as a bestseller in Women's Poetry. If I were advertising a poetry book using a category ad, I may show against that grossly misclassified title. A customer could click on my book out of curiosity but it's unlikely to convert to a sale. This helps to make category ads for books sometimes awfully expensive, as each click costs money.

Recommendation: Think of category ads as similar to auto ads. Use them with the intention of capturing good converting ASINs that you may not have otherwise found. Use them short term.

Overall, I am an enormous fan of product attribute capabilities for books and expect that Amazon is going to continue making its much-needed serious investment here.

Interest Targeting

This is currently only available for KDP authors via Lockscreen Ads. The "interest" targeting here means the genre. There are targeting capabilities for a subset of subgenres in the browse tree.

Negative Targeting

Standard targeting is all about trying to make positive connections. But life doesn't work out like that. What about damage control? What about brand safety? How do you ensure that your book ad doesn't show on the wrong page? Use negative targeting. You don't have to do this up front; you can add negative targets well after your campaign is live.

Negative keyword or product/ASIN targeting is used to block irrelevant traffic. It works by suppressing an ad from being shown to browsers that you deem to be wrong, even though they used similar search terms, based on your negative keywords. In other words, you believe the customer's intent was not to find a book like yours.

When you're creating a campaign, you will select your standard targets, your positive targets. Once you've entered your positive targets, you can then add negatives. For example, I want to target general contemporary romances and I'm starting with all three match types to see what results I get. But I know from the start that I don't want to pay for clicks by customers looking for "free" because my book is not free, so I add a bunch of free terms to my negative targets list.

When you're optimizing campaigns, *potential* negative targets may appear in the customer search term report. If you see targets incurring significant costs but are not converting into either sales or pages read, these are candidates to exclude. You can add them to your negative targets list and eliminate wasted spend, driving spend efficiency.

Recommendation: Review your reporting or dashboard, identify those terms that are not converting to sales or royalties, and move them to your negative targets list. If you don't want auto ads to spend on phrases related to your author or book name(s), add those terms as a negative.

Targeting on the Horizon

There's another interesting type of targeting that is available outside of KDP advertising. Other advertiser types, notably sellers and vendors, have access to an ad type called Sponsor Display (SD). Unfortunately it needs to be brought to a better state before it rolls out to KDP authors as it is currently inconsistent and rife with hiccups. There are options to both on and off Amazon using custom-built audiences or pre-built Amazon audiences based on lifestyle, interests, life events and in-—market activities. Should they decide to roll it out to authors, I would expect major modifications to be able to consistently deliver results in books

Targeting is the area where you will need to invest time in preparing to advertise and requires experimentation to get it right. Expect to experiment 2-3 months when starting out. Keep these tactics in mind as you build out a master targeting list (Chapter 12).

CHAPTER 6
CAMPAIGN STRUCTURE

A **campaign** is not the ad itself. It's a set of ads sharing a budget. Each campaign consists of one or more ad groups containing the ads. I think of it as a filing system, with each level having its own set of controls. It's the place where you will store your important files – in this case, your ads. The ads dashboard is effectively the file cabinet, with portfolios being the file drawer. In the file drawer, you have several hanging folders, each representing a campaign. Within that hanging folder or campaign, there is a set of manila folders that are ad groups. Within those ad groups you have papers that are your ads or the ad *bundles*, each page having an advertised book+target+bid.

Portfolios

Portfolios are optional and are only supported in Sponsored Products at this time. You can use a portfolio as a file drawer to hold multiple campaigns, organizing them any which way you like. You can group your campaigns by pen name, series, book, season, theme, new releases, or anything that applies to the way you manage your catalog and author business.

Using portfolios allows you to filter your dashboard to only see campaigns within that portfolio. Doing so can help you more easily find where you need to dig deeper. You can further control your spending by creating budget caps at the portfolio level and streamline your billing so that you get a separate line item. If you don't group your campaigns into portfolios, the invoices will be a list of campaign-level line items and their spend.

Campaigns

Campaigns are the primary line item on the main ads dashboard for all ad types. They are often referred to as your "ads", although your ad lives lower in the campaign structure. As we learned in Part 2, your ad is the combination of the book+targeting+bid (and, of course, any relevance or other calculation that Amazon applies to it).

Ad Groups

An ad group is a collection of ads that share similar targets. Ad groups help you organize your ads or keywords by a common theme under one campaign umbrella.

Ad groups are new(ish) in the Amazon ads world, but they've been a way of organizing ad campaigns in Google for years. Currently, they're only available in Sponsored Products. An ad group is quite literally a group, a segment, or a bucket of similar targets.

For example, I have my account set up like this: file drawer = Portfolio = *New releases*. I have grouped my launch campaigns so I can track typical spend and performance trends in one place. The hanging folder = Campaign = *[book title]+SP+Auto+July21*. I specify the book title, ad type, targeting type and start month/year. The manila folder = Ad Group = auto. I'm naming the ad group a generic name because there is nothing specific I need to share. The paper = ad = target a, target b, target c...

Recommendation: Always use portfolios, when available, to better organize your ads. Use naming conventions for all layers of the campaign structure that allow you to understand what's working and what's not.

Tip: You can't delete portfolios. You can, however, rename them and move campaigns around.

CHAPTER 7
AD CREATIVE CUSTOMIZATION

The basic ad creative pulls from the Amazon catalog to display book cover, title, price, and star ratings. Each ad type has its own unique option to customize the ad with some sort of copy and/or image. Ad copy can serve as a teaser or the beginning of the pitch to buy.

Well-written copy can entice a customer to click the ad when the cover or title does not stand on its own. It gives readers one more data point on which they base their purchase (or, at least, click) decision, especially when all ad elements – the book cover, targeting, copy, and detail page – are aligned. Ideally it should help you to spend more efficiently. Once ads are created, it's not possible to either edit or to delete the customization from the ad.

Custom Text for Sponsored Products

Custom text is a feature within Sponsored Products that is only enabled for book advertisers (both KDP authors and publishers) in the US. The 150-character ad copy appears on product detail pages as a vertical block of italics beneath the cover and title, and as a horizontal block when shown within search results.

You can use the same custom copy for both digital and print copies of a title, but you cannot use it to advertise a group of books or series in a multi-ASIN campaign. Although Amazon defaults to custom text for KDP authors, this decoration is an optional feature. The custom copy is not search-indexed and does not influence metadata, therefore, does not impact ad sourcing or directly influence ad relevance. It is purely decoration to the customer.

New authors are easily side-tracked by trying to create the right custom copy. They wind up creating many ads to test this when, in fact, testing different ad creative on the same book and targets is technically impossible. This is because there is no such thing as A/B testing for this feature or anywhere else within Amazon Ads. What does that mean and why should you care? In marketing, A/B testing is when you have two variations of an ad and you put them out in the wild to determine which one performs better. However, by design, Amazon won't pull two of the ads, with the same targets at the same time or display at the same rate. One is going to win out for the ad placement more often meaning that one ad will just get more time in front of the customer. It's not a valid test and gives a false signal.

This is a noisy distraction when the author would be better served learning the ad mechanics that will increase relevant impressions.

Recommendation: Start ads without custom text, in order to get a solid grasp on how the mechanics of ads work. Once you have solid targets and want to drive more qualified click through, you may want to introduce custom text.

Headline & Image for Sponsored Brands

The ad creative for Sponsored Brands displays horizontally at very the top of a search; in fact, really *above* organic search results. Three books are shown and will display simultaneously. Also included is a 50-character custom headline along with an author photo (400x400 png, jpg or gif).

Custom Copy for Lockscreen Ads

Lockscreen Ads can include 50–150-character copy to accompany your book image.

Tip: To create the best custom copy, be sure to comply with the Guidelines, paying particular attention to spelling and grammar. Ensure your custom text is relevant to your targeting and enticing enough for a click. Amazon does not have data on this (because it's only a decoration) but you can find best practices on Bookbub's marketing pages.

CHAPTER 8
ALL ABOUT BIDDING

A **bid** is the highest price that you're willing to pay for a single click on your ad. This value will be sent into an auction where you'll compete with other eligible ads for readers' eyes. Your actual cost-per-click is determined in the auction. It doesn't mean that you'll always pay that amount of your bid, but it should be your ceiling. For example, if I set a bid for $.45, that means that I am willing to pay up to $.45 when a browser clicks on my book ad. You can set higher bids for targets that you think may be more valuable and lower bids on targets that you're unsure about.

Standard auction ("second priced auction"): from bid to cost-per-click

The **auction** is the process that happens when Amazon needs to decide which ad to show to a reader at a given time during their search or browsing journey. Each time an ad is eligible to appear for a customer, multiple ads will be "sourced" from the pool, vetted and go through the ad auction. This determines whether or not the ad is actually shown and to whom and where it will show.

If your bid wins the auction, you'll be charged $0.01 more than the second-highest bid in the auction for a click, but only up to your maximum bid amount. For example, if you bid $0.25, and next highest bid is $0.23, you'll win the auction and your cost-per-click will be $0.24.

Target Level Bid Types

There are three different bid types that you can apply to your ads at the target level:

Default bid: the base bid that will apply to all of your targets as the default when you don't apply a suggested bid or a custom bid. It's your fallback bid in the event you don't select the other bid options.

Suggested bid: a value calculated from recent winning bids. Amazon help content says this is recommended for new advertisers. I strongly disagree. They are just too wacky to be trusted to be a bidding starting point. For example, I'll see a bid suggested range of .02-.54, with a suggestion for me of .20. Yet somehow I can't get an impression for less than .65. Sometimes it's a much more dramatic – and expensive – range. Or the suggestions are not populated at all.

Custom bid: allows you to set the bids for some or all of your target. This requires a balancing act and requires vigilance to maintain it.

Recommendation: Set your own default bid. If you want to apply a custom bid, make sure you have your desired default set (rather than Amazon's). Don't start out applying suggested bids, but do keep an eye on them and use them when you're optimizing later. Be very careful to doublecheck your individual bids before you launch your campaign. The campaign builder flow is such that many authors believe they applied a default bid when, in fact, they accidentally assigned a different (higher) bid. Pay close attention!

How much should I bid?

This is a popular question, with a difficult answer because it's different for every individual and every book. Below are two bidding methods to consider. Assess which camp you (and your financial tolerance) fall into.

Fail Fast Method. This is a strategy employed by tech companies to drive experimentation quickly. Fail Fast for ads means bidding high with a campaign budget high enough to warrant a healthy click volume. For example, I'm bidding over the suggested range – perhaps $1.12 - for a strong target. I don't want to pay that much, but I want to ensure that I'm getting impressions from the beginning. I'm thinking that I "need" this target to take off. I know it's an expensive click, but I'm betting that I'll get meaningful return. Besides, my daily budget is capped sufficiently enough to avoid insane runaway spend.

This approach assumes that you're getting impressions if the book is relevant to the target; if it's not relevant, you'll get that signal, too. That's ok. Some targets just will not work; you want that signal as fast as possible. Obtaining the impression volume is key to getting statistically significant data on what is working (and not working) for you. You open the floodgates and then can react quickly.

Slow Dial Method. This method starts bidding low, NOT CHEAP. By low, I mean $.50. You should know by now that setting a bid at $.50 doesn't mean you'll pay $.50. It means you could pay up to that amount if you're in a bidding war. If you start at that amount, you may need to increase the bid if you're not getting impressions. You continue to increase the bid if you don't get traction (impressions). The Slow Dial approach requires patience but it is a solid approach for those who are concerned about cost. Your budget can be on the lower side because it can cover a lot more clicks.

Bidding Beyond the Basics

Once you've been advertising a while, you will start to see which types of keywords are driving more value to you. From this, you may adjust your bids accordingly. Here are some common observations (that don't necessarily hold for everyone):

Your own **branded keywords** may be the least expensive because you should be the most relevant target for your own book. However, not all sales will be incremental; these clicks may already be in your funnel. See Chapter 20 for more information on self-defense brand targeting.

Category keywords are for those generically shopping in your genre. They may be more easily influenced, and in some categories, they drive the highest search volume. This means that these are often the most popular terms and can have high bids.

Best-selling authors can be expensive because there is fierce competition. They may not be the right targets if you don't have solid sales volume. Instead, aim for the mid-list authors.

Campaign Level Bid Modifiers

There are two tiers of bid controls at the campaign level (as opposed to the target level): (a) dynamic bidding strategies, and (b) bids by placement. These modifiers apply to the entire campaign including all ad groups within that campaign.

Bid Strategies

Bidding Strategies take every single target bid and apply a modifier, depending on your preference. There are 3 options here: fixed bids, dynamic down only, and dynamic up and down. You are required to set a bid strategy preference when you create a campaign.

Fixed Bidding

Fixed bidding is straightforward and means, "Hey, don't touch my bid." Amazon will send your exact bid into the auction. Fixed bidding is recommended if you need to keep your math simple and want to just understand the bare-bones relevance of your target.

Dynamic bidding

Dynamic bidding leverages Amazon's machine learning to determine your likelihood of a sale (against that target). Based on that determination, it may increase or decrease the actual bid that goes to auction. Amazon is trying to predict the success of your click. Remember here that this is an algorithm that is agnostic. It is *not* exclusively for books, so it is more about sales than borrows or pages read.

What factors do they look at in books to determine the probability of conversion to a sale? This is constantly changing, and I'd be hard pressed to find anyone at Amazon who could provide a clear answer. These are some of the elements they *could* look at to determine the probability of a sale:

1. the relevance of your ad to your target
2. the history of your ASIN – how well your book has been selling
3. the engagement with your book detail page – how many people review your book detail page vs buy the book or add it to a wish list
4. the history of the ad itself
5. the ad CTR history
6. the rate of page visits to conversion.

Note that I did not include sales rank because it's not an output metric. That is not a direct input here, but there are factors from sales that will go into the determination of relevance.

Within dynamic bidding there are two options: 'down only' or 'up and down'.

Down only

A bid with "down only" strategy goes to the second-price auction as normal, but Amazon will assess the ad's propensity to convert to a sale. If Amazon believes it's less likely to convert to a sale, your bid will be reduced in real time, regardless of what's happening at auction. This is a low-risk bidding tactic and is recommended when you want to test a higher bid than you're usually comfortable with. I used to recommend this because it's the way the auction ran prior to 2019. However, I see this constricting impressions, perhaps due to KU metrics.

Up and down

When you choose the 'up and down' strategy, Amazon will increase your bid when the ad is more likely to convert to a sale and decrease your bid when it's less likely to convert to a sale. While this is pretty straightforward, it can be difficult math for those trying to figure out their CPC and actual bids. It's hard to tell what you're actually going to be paying, and this could wildly fluctuate depending on your targets.

Adjust bids by placement

The second campaign-level bid modifier is optional: Adjust Bids by Placement, which was formerly known as "bid plus." This allows you to adjust your bid depending on whether the ad is served on Top of Search (TOS) or Product Page. In Sponsored Products, can you view your ad's performance by placement: Top of Search (first page), Product Pages, Rest of Search (middle or bottom). For ads that appear on the Top of Search and Product Pages, you may bid higher if you see it's converting well. While Amazon lists a performance break out for Rest of Search, there is no bid modifying capability available for that placement.

You may designate to bid a percentage higher (up to 100% higher on the first page of search results; 50% higher for other placements). Your bid is adjusted in proportion to the likelihood of conversion so you may get more conversions. This is recommended when you've been advertising for a while and when your appetite for risk is higher.

If your base bid is $.25, depending on your campaign bidding strategy, you will pay the following:

- campaign bidding strategy stays fixed – $.25
- campaign bidding strategy is down only – from $0 to $.25

campaign bidding strategy is up and down – up to $.50 (i.e. up to 100% above your base bid)

The Myth of the Highest Bidder

It's a common myth that the highest bidder wins the auction and an aggressive bid will win over a solid suggestion. This myth ignores the importance of **relevance**. A key tenet of Amazon is *customer obsession*, which means that Amazon is not going to allow a big spender to swoop in and take over ad slots unless it provides a meaningful experience for the customer.

The ads algorithm ingests signals demonstrating how customers feel about your book. This can be derived from how they engage with your ad and the book being advertised. These signals are essentially inputs to relevance. Relevance is key to winning ad placement, and you need to keep this top of mind as you determine your ad targets. While you do still need to bid competitively to win against other relevant authors, your presence on your targeted bookshelf should be meaningful – relevant – for customers.

Recommendation. Choose which type of bidder you think you are based on your financial tolerance for risk. If you're worried about spend and want to take a more conservative approach, use the Slow Dial method. Ignore suggested bids (I'll tell you later when to reference them during optimization). Set your own default bid to an amount you're comfortable with. Start off conservative but not cheap.

CHAPTER 9
ALL ABOUT BUDGETS

A **budget** is the amount you're willing to spend to advertise. You are required to set a campaign-level budget, which can be a daily budget or for the duration of your campaign. You may also choose to set an additional budget for a group of campaigns in a portfolio to further control your spending.

Budgets are soft caps on ad spend. Because ad impressions are not guaranteed, the consumption of that budget is not guaranteed. In other words, it's very likely that Amazon will not spend it all.

While you are required to set a campaign-level budget, there is an additional but optional spend control: a portfolio-level budget. There is no account-level budget option (which would be very helpful).

Campaign Budgets

How campaign budgets work

At the campaign level, a daily budget is the amount you're willing to spend on an ad each day. The daily budget is averaged over the course of a calendar month. On any day you could spend less than your daily budget, or up to 25% more than your average daily budget. At the end of the month, your total spend on a campaign should not be more than the daily budget you've set, multiplied by the number of days in that month. Remember that the budget is across 30 or 31 days, so you occasionally may see a spike over your daily budget.

Example: You set a $100 daily budget for July. $100 × 31 days = $3100 total potential spend for July. Some days, you're only spending $60, other days, you may spend $125 but your monthly spend will come in at $3100 or less.

What should my daily campaign budget be?

Sponsored Ads work with any budget that is more than the cost of a bid. Although theoretically you can set a daily budget as low as $5, in practice your ads will be throttled by your own doing. This means that they may not show up as frequently as you need them to in order to get some decent sales. With a $5 daily budget, if you also set a bid for $.25, you'll only get 20 clicks before you hit your budget. If that's the only level of risk you're able to take to start out, that's fine. But understand that this will have a very low impact on sales.

According to Amazon, on average, sellers who launch an ad campaign with a budget of at least $5 have up to **140% more ad-attributed sales** than those who set a budget lower than $5. You'll want to choose a budget that's high enough to help you reach your goals, but just how high that is will vary from advertiser to advertiser. In general, you'll see results—ad impressions, clicks, and sales—with a budget of just $10 a day.

Remember: Never set a daily budget you're not comfortable with. You can always start smaller and then invest more as you find what works best for your business. You can change your daily budget at any time, and the adjustments will take effect immediately in your campaign.

For more on allocating budget to your strategy, See Chapter 10.

Portfolio Budgets

Using a budget cap in a portfolio helps to further manage your ad spend. You can choose from three options for portfolio-level budget caps:

No budget cap. This is the default setting. Amazon only looks at your campaign level budget cap.

Recurring monthly budget cap. This is a portfolio budget that will reset the first day of each month.

Date range budget cap. If a portfolio budget is exhausted, all campaigns associated with that portfolio will be paused, even campaigns that still have budget remaining.

For example, imagine that campaign A has a lifetime budget of $500, campaign B has a lifetime budget of $500, and the portfolio budget is $750. When the total spend of both campaigns reaches the $750 portfolio budget limit, all campaigns in the portfolio will be paused. If campaign A reaches its lifetime budget of $500, campaign B can spend $250 until it reaches the portfolio's budget cap.

Recommendation: Use a monthly portfolio level budget by series or title or other marketing theme. Know that Sponsored Brands and Lockscreen Ads do not yet support portfolios, so this budget cap will only apply across your Sponsored Products campaigns.

Campaign Budget Rules

Budget rules may be set at the campaign level, allowing you to designate exceptions to your regular daily budgets. You may set them for a particular date range to increase your budgets when traffic is expected to increase (for example, Black Friday Cyber Monday) or you may set them based on campaign performance as ACOS, CVR, or CTR.

This feature is designed for more sophisticated advertisers who understand what is working in their ads. Authors should be careful when setting these budget exception rules: the performance rules based on sales (ACOS, CVR) will not include pages read. While the CTR rule may be useful, you should still be evaluating success at your target level. You could still have a very high CTR on a target that is not converting to pages read or sales.

On existing campaigns, click into the campaign and on the left navigation bar you'll see a "Budget rules" section. Here you can add a rule to allow you to bid higher at peak times. The pre-populated Recommended Events are Halloween, Black Friday and Cyber Monday (BFCM). Note that Black Friday and Cyber Monday are listed as separate events, even though they stretch into one long peak buying season. Use this seasonal option with caution as there may be more clickers poking around looking for good ideas.

Recommendation: Make these two adjustments on any campaign that is spending efficiently (in other words, non-converting targets have been removed and bids are profitable): (1) set a longer date range than BFCM and (2) make sure you create your own timeframe for the digital peak occurring in late December through late January. This peak typically starts on 12/26 when customers may have new Kindle devices. Obviously, this is especially helpful if you are in Kindle Unlimited.

In general, don't be too quick to listen to the budget increase recommendations, which are often stale (especially if you're monitoring and adjusting your campaigns frequently). Amazon teases you with estimated missed clicks and impressions, but it doesn't share any context on the conversions. You need conversion intel to be able to act on a budget recommendation. The same advice also applies to your budget recommendation emails and your dashboard notifications. Tip: Using the Budget Rule feature does not make your ads "set it and forget it." You still need to keep monitor spend!

PART III
PREPARING TO ADVERTISE

Take some time to prepare for advertising and do an audit of your product. This time is an investment that will go a long way towards running successful ads and reducing the time it takes to manage them. Draft a loose plan and audit your project to confirm you're ready to go. Don't just assume that since you've published with no issues, you're safe. If you uncover cracks in your foundation, address critical issues prior to advertising. Make sure your foundation can support the extra attention you're about to receive. Failing to do so risks customer trust that you can't win back.

CHAPTER 10
DEVELOP YOUR ADS STRATEGY

Strategy can sound daunting, as if it needs to be perfect and groundbreaking. It doesn't, so let's pause that kind of thinking right now. Your strategy doesn't have to be set in stone; instead, look at this as a living, working plan.

Randomly running lots of ads with lots of uncurated keywords is not a strategy. Having a goal helps you to make certain advertising decisions with less effort. Asking yourself, "Does this align to my strategy?" is the mechanism for simplification. It will help set the right expectations and lay the groundwork for ad maintenance (a/k/a optimization).

Your ads plan should address these components: Product, Audience, Timing, Tactics, Budget.

Strategies are conceived around unique variables, so there won't be a single "just do this" detailed tactical plan that works for everyone or every title. Instead, use this as more of a top-level checklist. Once you've done the work and you're building campaigns in the ads console, you'll still be making campaign-level decisions, but this high-level strategy will help inform those decisions. As you continue to advertise (and write more), your priorities will evolve over time.

1. Prioritize Your Product and get Advertising Ready

You'll need to prioritize which titles in your Amazon catalog you'd like to promote. This is easy if you have one or two books. It can be more challenging if you have a larger series, multiple series, or a catalog of unrelated books. There are different approaches to consider. You may want to focus only on your top sellers to push them even higher, advertise the first in series on all books, focus on strictly new releases, or run ads across all titles.

Once you know which titles you will advertise, you'll need to audit the product. See Chapter 11, Advertising Ready.

2. Find Your Audience

For your book to gain attention, it's imperative to understand your audience within the Amazon context. Where does your book fit on the virtual bookshelf? Think about the logical search behavior customers may use to get there. Start documenting your findings. Look at which tropes or genre terms organically show your book in Amazon's search results. Do this exercise for your comp titles and then study bestsellers in your sub-genre.

Unlike keywords for retail, you can afford to be much broader if you'd prefer, or you can go narrow and very specific. Whichever path you choose, make sure to start with the ideal targets and work backwards. This is the area where it will take some time for you to build a master targeting list. It does not have to be perfect. It's a starting point for your ads. See more on Building a Master Targeting List in Chapter 12.

3. Plan Your Timing

I encourage you to ignore any financial constraints when first planning. Instead, think about the ideal state for the upcoming year. Your schedule should tie back to how you prioritized your catalog. Will you be focusing on first in series? If so, then that's an evergreen, which is an always-on ad. You won't need to do much fancy calendaring. If you're going to focus on new releases, think about your planned release dates for the year. Layer on seasonality that's appropriate for your genre, including popular shopping holidays. For a non-fiction writer, perhaps industry events related to your area of expertise are important for your book sales or your greater author brand. If so, you can layer that on your ads schedule as well.

Recommendation: Prepare to always advertise at peak times when most people are browsing. Amazon's high traffic times are roughly Q4 into the end of January; however, "Q4 holiday" traffic starts lifting towards the end of September.

4. Consider Available Tactics

Everything you've thought about prior is an input to tactics. What tools do we have to actualize this strategy? First look to the ad types. Each ad type has a different level of visibility and available inventory throughout the customer search and browse journey. Do you have a use case for one or more?

Based on your targeting research, you can think about which targeting tactic to employ: ASIN targeting, keyword targeting, category targeting. Your research should have yielded information on all three.

Bidding is also a tactic. If you are a new author, you'll want to start simple and steer clear of most of the fancier bidding tools in the console. When thinking about bids, if you are an existing series author, you need to calculate the value of a reader (read through). See Leveling Up, Chapter 20.

Thinking about these tactics now will prepare you and prevent you from getting stuck when you're actually creating campaigns in the Amazon Ads campaign builder.

5. Allocate an Advertising Budget

"What should I spend on ads?" is a common question with no one set answer. Your strategy should help influence this, but you should also consider the financial risk you are willing to take based on personal circumstances.

If you're just starting out with ads, you'll need to determine a monthly budget for a three month initial investment. This number will need to be divided amongst your campaigns. This is true regardless of where you are in your author journey. Ad success will take time, and often the first few months are spent experimenting to see what works for a particular book.

Recommendation: As a new author, set aside three months of ad budget, then re-evaluate. It doesn't have to be a big number, but you'll need to spread it across multiple campaigns, and it will need to be enough for a reasonable daily budget. For example, if you can spend $500 in month 1, that would break down to just under $17 per day. That $17 needs to be spread across multiple campaigns, so this will limit how many you can run. That's ok; just know that up front.

If your books are already materially selling, use x% of previous month's sales.

If your book sales are sluggish and you're not even breaking even, again, think about your appetite for risk. Can you afford to allocate $500/month for three months? If you are starting with less than $300/month allocated, know ahead of time that it's going to take longer to move along that learning curve.

Experienced authors can consider an annual media plan based on previous year. Year over year performance is not always consistent, but this gives you a starting point. Allocate that against each quarter, considering the use cases that you're trying to cover with ads: some always-on ads, extra in peak seasons or according to your genre seasonality, pre-orders, new releases and your overall objective. Work out this number and write it down.

CHAPTER 11
ADVERTISING READINESS

Amazon employs models that calculate the propensity for customers to engage with products, analyzing multiple factors of product listings. This calculation determines a product's advertising readiness. 'Advertising-ready products are 16 times more likely to be clicked on if advertised than non-advertising-ready products.'[1] While this data is not broken out for books specifically, applying this lens to your catalog ensures that you're on top of your game for prospective readers.

Title. Your title should make sense. Obviously in books, there is expected to be vagaries and nuance. If also using a subtitle, make sure it clarifies the title and leverages search engine optimization (SEO) principles that make sense for your book.

Cover Art. When your cover surfaces in search results in an ad displayed on a competitor's page, it needs to entice the reader to click. A weak cover can dissuade a prospective reader in a nanosecond if they see it, or they may gloss over your book missing it entirely. This may cause ads with impressions but no clicks. Design (including fonts) should be professional-looking and align with the expectations of your book and genre or subgenre. If you have a series, check for continuity across the series brand. Be sure to review the thumbnail version because many customers browse on mobile. This can have a significant negative impact on a cover legibility.

Look Inside the Book (LITB). This detail page feature allows customers to sample pages from your book. Peruse this to make sure that you are proud of what potential readers see! Re-read for clarity and typos. For print editions, Amazon indexes words from LITB content for search results. Make them count.

Blurb / Detail page description. The customer clicked on your ad primarily because the cover resonated with them. The point of the detail page copy is to validate that initial interest, converting to a sale or download. Use a strong headline. Hook the reader. While some customer decisions may be made less intentionally, the book description on the detail page is a more conscious input to a customer's decision to convert. The blurb should accurately describe what the reader can expect from your book. Aside from being a propellant to convert, this is one of the first steps in building the path to an excellent review later.

Pricing. Pricing your book should be a strategic decision rather than a random act. Some genres are more price sensitive than others. You can look at your comps and bestsellers in your genre. Note the differences between indies and traditionally published titles, and whether there is a trend towards Kindle Unlimited enrollment or not. You should know the standard pricing by format in your genre for indies. Pay less attention to traditional publishers unless that's your true comp set.

A+detail page content. This new creative feature takes up considerable real estate on your listing page, allowing you to share more content to lure readers to convert. While it's too new of a feature for books to have data, this creative slot is seen as a lever to increased conversion for other types of products. While this can be beneficial if you're really adding value to the detail page, there is also the possibility of stopping conversion if done incorrectly. When considering how you want to fill that space, remember that it displays above the book description on mobile devices. This means potential readers could make decisions based on that image rather than description plus image.

Star Ratings. If you have low star ratings, please re-consider advertising at this time. Fix the book or write another.

Reviews. Spend time with your reviews. Is there anything that you can improve? This is important to focus on if your first review showing is a negative one. Write down key themes, both positive and negative.

Review Your Metadata. Metadata is the engine under the hood that powers site traffic. Your metadata is first influenced by the information you include in your KDP book listing. (Amazon may create more metadata based on that.)

Retail suggestions and organic search results are influenced by metadata. This is how the most appropriate match is made between a potential reader and your book. This means it directly impacts your book discovery and, ultimately, your sales. Amazon will use the information provided in your ad to determine who to show it to, but this must align with the data in your book's listing.

Amazon retail may show your book to someone who searched for books within your category, but ads may dive even deeper and show it to readers who are statistically believed should be interested in your book. On top of that, the ads algorithm will look at not only interest, but propensity to convert to a sale. Metadata will include categories (genre and subgenre), keywords, title and subtitle. These are strong levers to your success as you enter this data in your KDP Title Setup.

I am highlighting here only the basics that I consider to be prerequisites for successful ads. They help users find your book when browsing the Amazon bookstore. The mission here is to have the right customer click on your ad, for that reader's expectations to be met by the book description, and for nothing to stand in the way of that customer converting to a reader. Do what you can to eliminate objections. Identify gaps and make improvements before you advertise.

1. https://advertising.amazon.com/en-us/resources/whats-new/advertising-ready-product-sort-sponsored-product

CHAPTER 12
KNOW YOUR CUSTOMER: BUILDING A MASTER TARGETING LIST

In the movie *Field of Dreams*, the main character says, "If you build it, they will come." That is an outdated fallacy that does not work well with today's more sophisticated public. This frame of mind leads to ideas like "training the reader to like this or do that," leaving you to wonder why your ads aren't performing or your books aren't selling. You're pushing where there's no demand.

A key mechanism employed at Amazon is 'Working Backwards.' No features are released to end customers, suppliers, or advertisers without going through a rigorous working-backwards exercise to confirm demand. This helps to vet what gets put out publicly.

The working-backwards method is like writing to market. It's not that you are selling out; instead, you are selling (or writing or advertising) to an expressed need. And you know your readers expressed this need because you've done your research. Adopting this framework for your targeting strategy ensures that you connect with readers where they are in their customer journey. You will not be out on the sidelines shouting "Hey, come over here!" while they engage with another book. Let's apply this to building your master targeting list.

Your ads will not run without the right targeting. The right targeting means targeting relevant to your book. Amazon deems an ad to be relevant if it wins the auction and gets an impression; the customer deems it relevant if they click on the ad. A high click-through rate signals strong relevance.

You can start off advertising – or start advertising a new title – by using a wide variety of targets, but it is likely that you will whittle them down to a few that work. Note that not all targets work all year round. For instance, I have seen authors having strong conversion on certain targets during the November and December gift-buying season, but who cannot get a single sale on that target the rest of the year. We hypothesize that this is due to the buying behavior of that particular genre during gift-buying season.

So, what *is* a master targeting list? This is simply a repository of all your different targets. You can keep this in Excel, Word, Pages, or whatever you prefer. To build your master list, put on your reader hat: Where do your readers spend time? Are they in Facebook groups devoted to the genre? Are they on Goodreads?

A quality master targeting list may include:

- competitive titles (actual book titles)
- competitive authors (author names)
- competitive ASINs
- competitive categories (remember to look at both Books and Kindle categories, as the browse trees can be different)
- categories/genres/sub-genres that are similar or adjacent to yours

- keywords or search terms that readers use to find books like yours
- common genre tropes
- popular characters or series
- general book terms
- your own brand terms – variations of your author name, your book titles, series names, and ASINs in all formats
- keywords sourced from your reviews

As you're creating this list, bucket them and label them. Be sure to include the source. You'll want to reference this later in the campaign or ad group name to help you better understand what's working amongst your campaigns.

Strive for a well-rounded mix of head terms and long tail to ensure that you're really covering the purchase path and varied levels of shopper intent.

Head terms are usually one or two words. They are used by customers early in the purchase lifecycle. The conversion may not be as high immediately in a head term campaign. They are often used to drive discovery and brand awareness.

The master targeting list is not only for positive targets. It may wind up holding some negative targets as well. These are ones you'll ultimately exclude – either occasionally or always. An example of this would be your own brand terms. Sometimes you want to target them and sometimes you may not want to pay for clicks on your own brand names. For more about negative targeting and brand defense, see Chapter 5 All About Targeting and Chapter 20 Leveling Up.

When building your list, targeting resources are abundant yet too many authors rely on a single source or pay for a tool prematurely thinking it's a shortcut. Starting with free resources really puts you in the customer seat.

Within Amazon Ads

Solid targets can be found right within the advertising console. Amazon offers suggestions as you're building your campaign. This is a great starting point but make sure to curate them as the campaign builder sometimes tosses in junk terms. You don't want to spend on these! What are junk terms? You'll know them when you see them. For example, if you're advertising a book with "maid" in the title, "Halloween maid costume" may show up as a recommended target. Junk!

If you're already running ads, check your Search Term reports regularly. This report shows the specific customer search term that is matched to your target. Pull those customer search terms onto your master list.

On Amazon Retail Marketplace

If you play around in the retail marketplace as a customer, you can find targets related to your book from various sources.

Search and Browse. The first step is to search and browse in your genre. Notice that these are two different terms. Searching means actually putting a word or phrase in the search bar. If you start typing in keywords related to your book, you can see what autofill suggestions appear. Browsing refers to looking at the left navigation and clicking on a browse node (genre/subgenre/sub-subgenre). You'll notice different search results in the Books category vs the Kindle Store. Grab both formats. As you search and browse, notice who's advertising throughout your experience. If it's relevant and your book will make a good fit beside it, then add it to your list.

Amazon Publishing. Familiarize yourself with what's being published and promoted by Amazon Publishing (A-Pub). A-Pub titles are corporate big bets that should be sure to get significant traffic.

Bestsellers. Amazon bestseller charts include most read, most sold, free, paid, best books of the month, etc. It's always great to include known high-traffic ASINs. But don't just grab the entire list – curate it, ensuring that you have the right books and not a set of misclassified junk.

Off Amazon

Reader behavior off of Amazon can also give insight into how customers shop for books and what targets you can use to get readers to find you. Consider where readers congregate to chat about books and make wish lists, 'best of' lists and niche interest lists. This could be at reading-specific websites, like Goodreads, Libby, and BookRiot, libraries, or major newspapers sites. Subscribe to newsletters like BookBub to see which promoted titles in your genre are likely to get a surge of traffic. Add these to your list.

Tip: See also the third party tools that help with keyword research in Chapter 23.

PART IV
INTRODUCING THE ADS DASHBOARD

We've arrived at the ads dashboard or ads console. Let's do a quick walk through before we get started with campaign building.

CHAPTER 13
THE ADS DASHBOARD

This chapter provides an overview of your ads account and highlights key customization and other features that you may need. You may not want to read this now, but if you can't tackle a function, you can refer back to this chapter.

In your account, the main dashboard will be in a large, light grey (off-white) box. This is the campaign manager. This is where all your core campaign action will display and where you will go to monitor ads. If you have not yet created any ads, you should see "choose your campaign type" and three blocks, one each for each of the ad types.

Above the large box is a horizontal blue strip – your top navigation bar. This is for personal preferences like your account name (which you can customize), marketplace, and language. It is where you can also access written help content and contact support, should you need to.

From the left vertical navigation bar, you can click to your main campaign manager, and view reporting, access billing and payments, and visit support center, training courses, and KDP.

Customizing Account Name

On the top right-hand side you should see your account name and the country location, with a little arrow indicating that there's a drop-down menu. If you have not named your account, it will read "Sponsored Ads – KDP".

Recommendation: Change that to an account name that's meaningful for you.

Changing Default Language

If you need to change the default language on your account, it's easy to do so from the top navigation bar of your ads console. To the far right you should see a small person icon. Clicking on that reveals your ad identification: the name of your ads account and the primary email address associated with that account. You can switch accounts if needed, and you can also change your language. From time to time, the default language on your account may accidentally change and you'll need to refresh it to your native language. Currently there are 10 languages available.

Recommendation: Make sure your account has the right language preference set. This will impact dashboard and email communication.

Customizing Communications

In the top right corner of the ads console, click on the user icon. Below the language switcher, you'll see the communication settings towards the bottom. This is where you can manage the notifications that you receive on this account. You can designate whether you want notifications by email, text or in-app. Notifications are broken out by product, news events, education training, campaign recommendations, new marketplace recommendations, surveys and promotional offers.

Recommendation: At minimum, be sure to have notifications on for product news and education and training.

Toggling Between Marketplaces

Many authors have multiple accounts worldwide. The accounts are linked by region. This means that if you have a US account, you can easily toggle to your Canadian account. Similarly, if you have a United Kingdom account, you can easily toggle to your accounts in Germany, France, Italy and Spain (clearly this was a pre-Brexit decision). To do so, click the drop-down arrow beside your account name and locale. Doing so reveals the different countries where you have already established accounts.

Finding Official Help Content

To the right of the bell, you'll see a question mark in a circle, representing "Help." Clicking on it opens a new tab with the Help content so you don't need to worry about losing your place in the ads dashboard. You can search help topics using the search bar here. Towards the bottom of this page, you will also see your case log if you have created any cases or have contacted the ads team.

Housekeeping and Account Hygiene

Think about how you want to organize your campaigns and how you may want to name them. You'll thank yourself for doing this early on. Your dashboard can get messy! Dashboard organization is not Amazon's strong suit. You cannot delete or hide old campaigns. This means your dashboard will soon get overloaded, and it may be tough to sort through and/or track.

Tip: Keep your credit card up to date. When issues with credit cards arise, ads may take some time to restart as it takes a while to propagate the billing system.

Naming Campaigns

When you think about naming campaigns, think about what you'll need to know later. Use a simple standard campaign naming convention to help you understand reporting and more easily identify campaigns when you do optimization work later.

Example: [book name] + [targeting type] + [targeting theme] + [bid strategy]

Hpotter KW manual broad high

[Book] + [keyword theme] + [bid strategy]

Hpotter Kw comp author dynamic up

You can also use that same type of naming convention – or a similar one – at the ad group level.

Notifications

On the top right of your dashboard to the right of your account name, you should see the bell icon. Clicking on this will reveal notifications (you may not have any at this time). For example, Amazon will notify you if a campaign is going out of budget.

Managing Users

At some point, you may wish to have another person work on your account on your behalf or with you. It's easy to do this. Go to left navigation and click Administration, "access and settings". From there you should easily see the button "invite a user". You will need to enter their username and email address. Unless you want the person responsible for billing, or to have access to your credit card, I highly suggest that you remain the admin on the account and only invite additional users as editors. Recently, Amazon has expanded the access options and you can also customize these.

Tip: If you have multiple ads accounts, you can link them by inviting them to the other account. That way you can easily toggle back and forth between accounts instead of signing out and signing in repeatedly to change accounts.

CHAPTER 14
CREATING AN AD

Let's put all the ad concepts that we've learned so far to use and start creating manual campaigns. This is my standard way of creating the first set of manual campaigns. (The first auto campaign is covered for barebones beginners in Chapter 0.)

Setting Up Sponsored Products Campaigns

To get started with Sponsored Products, have the following on hand: the ASINs that you want to advertise (this can either be the actual Amazon product identifier or it can be the book title), your budget amount, and your master targeting list.

SP Campaign setup: Manual Keyword Targeting

Starting at the main campaign dashboard, click "create campaign". Next choose your campaign type -- sponsored products –and continue.

1. *Fill in a campaign name.* Create a campaign name overriding the default. The naming convention should be meaningful and help you later when you are trying to monitor or optimize campaigns. My go-to campaign naming convention is [book name]+ [ad type]+targeting+[date]. Using this book as an example, the campaign name would be "AA+SP+Man+KW Comp Auth+July21." Here I included the targeting that includes both the tactic and the fact that I'm using comp authors.
2. *Set start and end dates.* The default start date is the current date, but you can set a date to start running the ad in the future. You can keep the end date set to none or choose your own end date. I do not set end dates.
3. *Set a daily budget.* I recommend starting with a daily budget of $10 a day, if you can. Anything less than $10 will make it difficult to capture the volume of data that we need to get by running our first campaign.
4. *Choose targeting typ*e. Select manual. This means that you are doing the work to select targets.
5. *Select campaign bidding strategy.* Select fixed bids. These are known to drive a higher volume of impressions, which is what we are after in our first ad(s) because we want to get data. I cover the different bidding strategies in full in Chapter 8.
6. You can ignore the adjustments by placement at this point. However, sometimes the console defaults to a

10% increase, so double check that the percentages in each of those boxes equals zero.
7. *Select ad format.* Click the radio button to select Standard Ad, until you have nailed your targets and are certain you want to do custom copy.
8. *Name your ad group.* Even though we are only creating one ad group for this campaign, Amazon is creating an ad group on your behalf. There is no need to name it.
9. *Select products to advertise.* Select one book that you want to advertise and click "add." I suggest advertising both eBook and pbook formats to get the most impressions for the book that you can. Customers can always decide which format they prefer directly from the shared detail page.
10. *Create targets.* For the targets, you can use Amazon's keyword suggestions or enter your own list from your master targeting list.
11. *Set bids.* The ads console will default to suggested bid. Using the drop-down, change that to default bid when starting. Choose an amount that you are comfortable with. This should be the highest price that you are willing to pay for a click on your ad. I suggest $.50 as a minimum starting point, with the expectation that you may need to increase once the campaign is live.
12. *Negative targeting.* Any term or product assigned here will be excluded from your ads targeting.
13. *Click launch.*

You ad will now go into review. On the ads dashboard, the campaign will show "delivering" but at the ad group level, you will see "pending review."

SP Campaign Setup: Manual Product Targeting

Starting at the main campaign dashboard, click "create campaign". Next choose your campaign type -- sponsored products –and continue.

1. *Fill in a campaign name.* Create a campaign name overriding the default. Using my standard example, mine would be AA+SP+Man+ASIN Comp Titles+July21." Here I included the targeting that includes both the tactic and the fact that I'm using comp ASIN.
2. *Set start and end dates.* No end date is recommended.
3. *Set a daily budget.* Try to start with $10/day.
4. *Choose targeting type.* Select manual targeting.
5. *Select campaign bidding strategy.* Select fixed bids.
6. *Select ad format.* Click the radio button to select Standard Ad.
7. *Name your ad group.* If you are only creating a single ad group, you do not need to name the ad group.
8. *Select products to advertise.* Add the books you'd like to advertise.
9. *Input targeting.* Much like in keywords, you have different options for getting the targeting live. Here you can select category or individual products. This is a true ASIN campaign so will select individual products. You can use Amazon's suggested products (suggestions change based on the ASIN you're advertising), you can search for products, (for instance I can search "Fireman romance" and get related titles) or enter a list of ASINs from your master targeting list.
10. *Set bids.* The ads console will default to suggested bid. Using the drop-down, change that to default bid when starting. Choose an amount that you are comfortable with. This should be the highest price that you are willing to pay for a click on your ad. I suggest $.50 as a

minimum starting point, with the expectation that you may need to increase once the campaign is live.
11. *Negative targeting.* Leave negative targeting blank.
12. *Click launch.*

You ad will now go into review. On the ads dashboard, the campaign will show "delivering" but at the ad group level, you will see "pending review."

SP Campaign Setup: Manual Category targeting

Starting at the main campaign dashboard, click "create campaign". Next choose your campaign type -- sponsored products –and continue.

1. *Fill in a campaign name.* Create a campaign name overriding the default. Using my go to naming convention, this would be AA+SP+Man +Cat Sci Fi Fantasy+July21."
2. *Set start and end dates.* The default start date is the current date, but you can set a date to start running the ad in the future. You can keep the end date set to none or choose your own end date. For your first campaign, make sure it is no less than one month out.
3. *Set a daily budget.* I recommend starting with a daily budget of $10 a day.
4. *Choose targeting type.* Select manual targeting.
5. *Select campaign bidding strategy.* Select fixed bids.
6. *Adjust bids by placement.* Ignore this for now.
7. *Select ad format.* Click the radio button to select Standard Ad.
8. *Name your ad group.* Even though we are only creating one ad group for this campaign, Amazon is creating an ad group on your behalf. There is no need to name it unless will be creating multiple ad groups.

9. *Select products to advertise.* Select the books you'd like to advertise.
10. *Select targeting.* Choose Product Targeting.
11. *Input targets.* Rather than individual products, select Categories (the default). Amazon will populate suggestions based on your book's metadata. You may further refine based on star rating, price and prime shipping. Some categories offer options for further genre refinements.
12. *Set bids.* The ads console will default to suggested bid. Using the drop-down, change that to default bid when starting. Choose an amount that you are comfortable with. This should be the highest price that you are willing to pay for a click on your ad. I suggest $.50 as a minimum starting point, with the expectation that you may need to increase once the campaign is live.
13. *Negative targeting.* Leave negative targeting blank for now.
14. *Click launch.*

You ad will now go into review. On the ads dashboard, the campaign will show "delivering" but at the ad group level, you will see "pending review."

Setting Up Sponsored Brands

To get started with Sponsored Brands, have the following on hand: at least 3 ASINs that you want to advertise (this can either be the actual Amazon product identifier or it can be the book title), an author photo, a 50 character headline and your master targeting list.

As a reminder, SB does not support ad groups or bidding strategies. There are no automatic campaigns.

SB Campaign setup: Keyword Targeting

Starting at the main campaign dashboard, click "create campaign". Next choose your campaign type -- sponsored brands –and continue.

1. *Fill in a campaign name.* Create a campaign name overriding the default. The naming convention should be meaningful and help you later when you are trying to monitor or optimize campaigns. My go-to campaign naming convention is [series]+[ad type]+targeting+ [date]. Using this book as an example, the campaign name would be "BGM+SB+KW Comp Authors+July21."
2. *Set start and end dates.* The default start date is the current date, but you can set a date to start running the ad in the future. You can keep the end date set to none or choose your own end date. For your first campaign, make sure it is no less than one month out.
3. *Set a daily budget.* SB offers either a daily or lifetime budget. I recommend starting with a daily budget of $10 a day.
4. *Select products to advertise.* You need to select a minimum of three books. Ensure that they are related, as in a collection or series.
5. *Add author photo.* Upload your author photo (minimum 400x400px PNG, JPG, or GIF, less than 1MB). Once you do this, it will remain in your account's creative asset library for future use.
6. *Confirm order of products.* Review the ad preview and confirm that you like the order of the products. If not, you may reorder them by dragging the book numbers.
7. *Write a headline.* Create a 50 character headline.
8. *Choose targeting type.* Select keyword targeting.
9. *Create targets.* For the targets, you can use Amazon's

keyword suggestions or enter your own list from your master targeting list.
10. *Select the match types.* I suggest starting with the default – all three match types.
11. *Set bids.* The ads console will default to suggested bid. Using the drop-down, change that to default bid when starting. Choose an amount that you are comfortable with. This should be the highest price that you are willing to pay for a click on your ad. I suggest $.50 as a minimum starting point, with the expectation that you may need to increase once the campaign is live.
12. *Negative targeting.* Leave negative targeting blank for now.
13. *Click launch.*

You ad will now go into review. On the ads dashboard, the campaign will show "delivering" but at the ad group level, you will see "pending review."

SB Campaign Setup: Product Targeting

Starting at the main campaign dashboard, click "create campaign". Next choose your campaign type -- Sponsored Brands –and continue.

1. *Fill in a campaign name.* Create a campaign name overriding the default. The naming convention should be meaningful and help you later when you are trying to monitor or optimize campaigns. My go-to campaign naming convention is [series]+[ad type]+targeting+[date]. Using this book as an example, the campaign name would be "BGM+SB+ASIN bestsellers+July21."
2. *Set start and end dates.* The default start date is the current date, but you can set a date to start running the ad in the future. You can keep the end date set to none

or choose your own end date. For your first campaign, make sure it is no less than one month out.
3. *Set a daily budget.* SB offers either a daily or lifetime budget. I recommend starting with a daily budget of $10 a day.
4. *Select products to advertise.* You need to select a minimum of three books. Ensure that they are related, as in a collection or series.
5. *Add author photo.* Upload your author photo (minimum 400x400px PNG, JPG, or GIF, less than 1MB). Once you do this, it will remain in your account's creative asset library for future use.
6. *Confirm order of products.* Review the ad preview and confirm that you like the order of the products. If not, you may reorder them by dragging the book numbers.
7. *Write a headline.* Create a 50 character headline.
8. *Choose targeting type.* Select product targeting.
9. *Input targeting.* This is a true ASIN campaign so select individual products. You can use Amazon's suggested products (suggestions change based on the ASIN you're advertising), you can search for products (for instance I can search "space pirates" and get related titles) or enter a list of ASINs from your master targeting list.
10. *Select the match types.* I suggest starting with the default – all three match types.
11. *Set bids.* The ads console will default to suggested bid. Using the drop-down, change that to default bid when starting. Choose an amount that you are comfortable with. This should be the highest price that you are willing to pay for a click on your ad. I suggest $.50 as a minimum starting point, with the expectation that you may need to increase once the campaign is live.
12. *Negative targeting.* Leave negative targeting blank.
13. *Click launch.*

You ad will now go into review. On the ads dashboard, the campaign will show "delivering" but at the ad group level, you will see "pending review."

SB Campaign Setup: Category targeting

Starting at the main campaign dashboard, click "create campaign". Next choose your campaign type -- sponsored brands –and continue.

1. *Fill in a campaign name.* Create a campaign name overriding the default. The naming convention should be meaningful and help you later when you are trying to monitor or optimize campaigns. My go-to campaign naming convention is [series]+[ad type]+targeting+[date]. Using this book as an example, the campaign name would be "BGM+SB+Cat Vampire Suspense+July21." I've included the specific category that I'm going to focus on for this campaign.
2. *Set start and end dates.* The default start date is the current date, but you can set a date to start running the ad in the future. You can keep the end date set to none or choose your own end date. For your first campaign, make sure it is no less than one month out.
3. *Set a daily budget.* SB offers either a daily or lifetime budget. I recommend starting with a daily budget of $10 a day.
4. *Select products to advertise.* You need to select a minimum of three books. Ensure that they are related, as in a collection or series.
5. *Add author photo.* Upload your author photo (minimum 400x400px PNG, JPG, or GIF, less than 1MB). Once you do this, it will remain in your account's creative asset library for future use.
6. *Confirm order of products.* Review the ad preview and

confirm that you like the order of the products. If not, you may reorder them by dragging the book numbers.
7. *Write a headline.* Create a 50 character headline.
8. *Choose targeting type.* Select product targeting.
9. *Input targets.* Rather than individual products, select Categories (the default). Amazon will populate suggestions based on your book's metadata. You may further refine based on star rating, price and prime shipping. Some categories offer options for further genre refinements.
10. *Set bids.* The ads console will default to suggested bid. Using the drop-down, change that to default bid when starting. Choose an amount that you are comfortable with. This should be the highest price that you are willing to pay for a click on your ad. I suggest $.50 as a minimum starting point, with the expectation that you may need to increase once the campaign is live.
11. *Negative targeting.* Leave negative targeting blank for now.
12. *Click launch.*

You ad will now go into review. On the ads dashboard, the campaign will show "delivering" but at the ad group level, you will see "pending review."

Setting up Lockscreen Ads

To create a Lockscreen Ads, have the following on hand: the ASIN you want to advertise and a 150 character headline. Due to the prominent location, Lockscreen has a stricter acceptance policy than other ad types. Read the Guidelines before creating an ad.

Starting at the main campaign dashboard, click "create campaign". Next choose your campaign type – Lockscreen Ads –and continue.

1. *Fill in a campaign name.* Create a campaign name overriding the default. The naming convention should be meaningful and help you later when you are trying to monitor or optimize campaigns. My go-to campaign naming convention is [book name]+ [ad type]+targeting+[date]. Using this book as an example, the campaign name would be "AA+LSA+Int Marketing+July21." This reflects that I'll be targeting the Marketing & Sales interest.
2. *Set start and end dates.* The default start date is the current date, but you can set a date to start running the ad in the future. I recommend running a one month campaign.
3. *Set a lifetime budget.* The minimum lifetime budget is $100. If running a one month campaign at $10/day (my usual budget for other ad types), I like to set $300 lifetime budget.
4. *Choose targeting type.* Select automatic targeting. Amazon will look at the data surrounding your book, select keywords and products that are similar to your book and target the ad against those.
5. *Select pacing.* You can run the campaign as quickly as

possible or pace it, spreading it out evening for the campaign duration. I choose the latter, spread evenly.
6. *Select product to advertise.* Choose which eBook you want to advertise. This ad type does not support multiple products in a campaign.
7. *Input interest targets.* Select your preferred targets. There are no suggestions made on your behalf.
8. *Set bid.* Set a single bid that will apply to every interest target. There is no option to customize per target or to apply bidding strategies.
9. *Enter custom text.* Write a 150 character blurb.
10. *Submit for review.*

You ad will now go into review. On the ads dashboard, the campaign will show "delivering" but at the ad group level, you will see "pending review."

Recommendation: Use Lockscreen Ads for new releases to complement your core Sponsored Products strategy. Because you cannot customize bids, run only one interest per ad.

PART V
MONITORING AND OPTIMIZING YOUR ADS

It's not a surprise to hear that many authors dislike math or even looking at spreadsheets. Yet self-publishing is an authorpreneurship, and there's no way getting around it. All advertisers should regularly monitor their ads. Not doing so puts you at risk of spending inefficiently. Others admit to digging into the metrics and analyzing performance in great detail. For that reason, I will present two ways of looking at your ads: a basic approach and a deep dive.

I'm taking off my white gloves here to share this opinion: it's clear that the ads team owning the console does not spend enough time with the tools they design. Whether you take the basic or deep-dive approach, monitoring campaigns is frustrating. Aside from the obvious (that ads take time, experimentation, and money), ads data points are all over the place. Some data is on the dashboard, while some data is in the reports. Reporting across products is not consistent. You can try to export the dashboard to simplify your process, but it only exports the one page you're viewing (not helpful if you have multiple pages of campaigns or targets) or won't include all the columns that you intended to export. For example, at the time of writing, KENP Pages Read and Royalties export into the wrong columns.

Offering a plethora of data is great, but the inconsistency makes it more challenging to assess what's working and what's not. This is akin to writing a book with a bunch of characters and disconnected scenes, leaving the reader to wonder "What's the story here?" Knowing the good, the bad and the ugly up front will remove at least some of the "Is it me?" worry. No, it's not you.

It helps to know what you can find where and have an understanding (even a "lite" understanding!) of some of the basic concepts. Whichever math/data camp you fall into, stay with me for the next two sections before skipping ahead to your chosen methodology.

CHAPTER 15
WHAT DATA IS AVAILABLE WHERE

The Ads dashboard displays high level metrics with the ability to "double click" to see more granular data. Running supplemental reports can be a supplemental deep dive activity.

Dashboard Reporting

The dashboard data is robust. Columns will default to a limited set; I recommend expanding those when you're first getting into a monetizing groove. In order to expand, just above the top column headers towards the right you'll see a "customize" button. Here you can select which columns you'd like to see. Select "all" and hit "apply".

The main campaign dashboard displays key campaign wrappings (targeting, portfolio, status) and reflects high level campaign performance metrics from impressions through conversions.

Dashboard Precision (or lack thereof)

Frustrated advertisers contend that ads dashboard data lacks integrity. This is fueled by some popular ads teachers who advise to completely ignore the dashboard because it's inaccurate. It's true that you may see campaign data for a particular day fluctuate. It's true that some metrics come in faster than others. It doesn't have the precision, but it's not *inaccurate*.

Impression and clicks (thus, CTR) should be accurate and timely[1] as these are purely captured by the ads system. Ad displays, user clicks (or not), ratio captured. The data is sent to the dashboard approximately every 12 hours. Although the data is sitting on your dashboard, Amazon is still reconciling the data through a process called traffic validation. Payment failures and orders that are cancelled within 72 hours will be removed from order totals. If Amazon detects unusual patterns in your data such as illegitimate, accidental or machine-generated clicks, they will remove it from your reporting. Most are removed within a day, but your data can fluctuate within the most recent three days.

A campaign's performance output metrics – conversion (sales, orders, pages read, KENP)-- rely on integration that reconciles retail customer behavior within a 14 day period (ads are on a last touch or last click attribution model[2]). The sales/pages read data may be different than your KDP dashboard which is likely to report sales as they come in.

Supplemental Reports

Additional reports are available for Sponsored Products and Sponsored Brands; there are no additional reports for Lockscreen. These reports are in the console but they are not on the main campaigns dashboard. You will need to run these reports separately from the left navigation bar. The reports help to understand trends as you look to identify what's working and what's not, and provide insight as to where you can make campaign adjustments. The reports across data are named inconsistently but do share a lot of the same metrics. Data retention differs across reports. Most of the report data is available for 90 days; the search term impression share report (SIS) retains data for the previous 65 days.

Although much of the same reporting may be available for both Sponsored Products (SP) and Sponsored Brands (SB), some of the report names differ. I've used the ad type abbreviations below to highlight the different names.

Search Term Report. Within each campaign, you'll see how your targeting and match type aligns with the customer search term. This is the greatest insight into customer behavior and what they type in the Amazon search box to find your ad. If you see an ASIN listed in your search term report (particularly in reports for automatic campaigns), it reflects the detail page where the ad surfaced (in the carousel); it's not that a customer searched for that alpha-numeric ASIN. This is my favorite report and the one I most frequently access.

Targeting (SP) and Keyword (SB) Report. The targeting report includes performance metrics for all targets that received at least one click. If you're getting impressions on targets but no clicks, that target will not be included in the report. (You can, however, see the impression volume by target on the campaign dashboard.)

Advertised Product Report. The advertised product report shows sales and performance metrics for by ASIN ads that received at least one impression. Use this if you have a messy console or need to remember what books are running where, or what targets are running where. Run this periodically to audit potential duplicate targets.

Campaign Report (SB). The campaign report offers another view of your dashboard that includes targeting type and bidding strategy. This is my least used report. However, I may check quarterly to see about bid strategy trends.

Placement Report (SP). Placement gives visibility into where your ads are showing and compares performance in those placements. When you're ready to optimize, this helps you determine whether you should start using the "bid by placement" feature. You may want to leverage this if you have a catalog of 25+ titles to understand the trend, if any. Otherwise, for weekly monitoring, I use the dashboard to view performance by placement.

Campaign Placement Report (SB). Similar to SP Placement report.

Keyword Placement Report (SB). Similar to the SP placement report, but at a keyword level.

Performance Over Time Report (SP). This is a very basic overview of all campaigns over time. You can see campaigns for up to 18 months. I don't spend much time here. I don't find it to be a very unique for of campaigns with anything that I feel is actionable.

Search Term Impression Report. This shows your impression share relative to all other advertisers on a target. I use this to better understand my bidding. If I see my search impression share is low on a target, I know there is room to grow. If I'm already getting the impressions, increasing the bid should drive growth. Depending on click volume, it may not mean I need to increase the budget. If a high share of impressions, I don't have a serious growth opportunity.

Budget report. The Budget report shows how your campaign performance may be impacted when your campaigns are out of budget. In my mind, I file this along with out of budget email notifications: raising the budget doesn't mean the conversion will occur at the same rate or even close. Budget increases are still recommended when there is no conversion.

Running Reports

To find the supplemental reports, go to the far left vertical navigation and click on the icon showing the bar graph. If you hover over it, you'll see that this is the Reports tab. Click the "Create Report" button and you'll see report options for Sponsored Products and Sponsored Brands.

Recommendation: Choose a time unit – I would start at monthly. This will give you a report from the last 30 days, but you can access data up to the last 90 days. I recommend scheduling for these to be emailed to you on a recurring basis so you can retain your data that may disappear from the console.

---

1. Given, of course, that there are no major outages.
2. This means that a user's last click is what gets attributed to the sale. Even if a user clicks on an ad, that user's sale may not get attributed to that click.

CHAPTER 16
MAKING SENSE OF METRICS

Making sense of all the data available can make your brain spin. **If that's you, know that all data points are not important all the time.** Allow me to introduce you to the concept of a metrics waterfall. Hopefully applying this waterfall view will help you conceptualize the data in a useful way that demystifies the metrics.

The Waterfall

When Amazonians look at data, they typically look at pages and pages of metrics. It's easy to get lost in the many different datapoints. You might feel the same when you look at your dashboard, especially if you have a lot of campaigns or books in your catalog or if numbers are not your thing.

When I first started at Amazon, my eyes glazed over during my first weekly metrics review. The metrics "deck" was printed back then and was *thick*. It was daunting until I understood the waterfall model. Ad metrics act like a waterfall, with water pooling at the top of the mountain and cascading down the ads pipeline until it reaches its destination.

In your advertising, the water pools up at the top with all tactics you used to create your campaign. They pool to drive impressions sitting at the very top of the waterfall. If the current picks up (via customer interest), impressions will cascade downward (or, in the ads dashboard, horizontally across columns), with clicks flowing through to conversions (sales or pages read). That's where we all want to be: swimming under the waterfall (it's warm, clear blue water) enjoying the fruits of our labor.

The waterfall is a way of looking at metrics to indicate how key performance actions and customer interactions with ads cascade down to the pool of orders, sales, pages read, and royalties. Conversions accumulate at the bottom of the pool in your waterfall only if you have sufficient current at the top. It's imperative for you to find a way to open the tap and drive impressions.

Metrics Inputs, Outputs & Levers

When pouring over these metrics decks, we also talked a lot about inputs and outputs, and what we had control over. As an author advertising, what are your *controllable inputs*? For each of the metrics, that answer can be different.

This input/output view is the framework we're going to apply to optimizing your ads, whether you're planning to take the basic dashboard approach or the deep-dive approach. This is how you should think about all the data within your account.

To break it down, we classify metrics: there are input metrics and there are output metrics. Input flows through to the outputs. So, when a problem is spotted in the form of a weak metric or something unexpected (for example, high impressions but low CTR), we ask: what are the *controllable* inputs?

Input Metrics

The two clearest controllable inputs in your ads waterfall are impressions and your CTR. You may be tempted to focus on sales or ACOS, but that's too far down the waterfall. Remember, you first need to drive the current! But ACOS can be a trigger signaling something awry in your campaign setup. What you really need to do is to look upstream and focus on the inputs at the top of the waterfall. This means impressions and CTR.

Levers

Your input metrics are actionable. There is a lever to dial up or down the metric.

Impressions: Your levers are bids and targets. This means that dialing bids up/down or increasing/decreasing the volume of targets should directly impact your impression volume. Bids should help grow impression possibilities on any relevant target. More targets should drive more impressions. Note that this is not infinitely true; adding another 2x targets will not give directly proportionate results. Your bid needs to be sufficient to allow Amazon to calculate how many clicks you could get with bid/budget and work backward to serve your ad. Obviously campaign budget will also impact impressions, but not so much where an artificially inflated budget (i.e., expressing a budget of $1000/day when you really only want to spend $25/day) will kickstart a low performing ad.

Clicks: Your primary lever is impression volume. You need impressions to get click volume. Your bids need to be competitive enough to win the auction and get the impression. Your budget needs to be competitive enough to support a high volume of clicks at a competitive cost-per-click. Relevance of your target should strengthen click volume.

CTR: Your lever is the quality of targets. If your CTR is too low, your targets are likely off. If it's a new title and Amazon gave it a "newly published" lift in visibility, at some point, Amazon may start pulling back on impressions if the CTR is low. Your campaign level CTR can be pulled down if you have one or two underperforming targets. This is where it's important to keep targeting lean, removing the dead weight of non-performing targets.

Using an inputs-outputs approach, you can focus your mental energy on what matters and reduce time staring at the dashboard.

Output Metrics

Output metrics are the results of the campaign. These are the conversions of your ad: orders, sales, pages read, and royalties. These are not directly controllable; instead, the expectation is that with the right inputs, you will have strong outputs. While you can make initial observations from reviewing outputs and, of course, you'll ultimately judge a campaign based on outputs, you'll focus your mind what you can do further upstream in the waterfall. We'll apply this in action during optimization.

CHAPTER 17
THE BASIC MONITORING APPROACH

This basic approach uses only the dashboard for both monitoring, analyzing and optimizing your campaigns. If you choose this path, you should realize that you will benefit most if you limit the volume of campaigns that you're running at any given time. Do not create a lot of campaigns at once.

Basic Monitoring for Auto Ads

If you are monitoring your first auto campaign that you just created while reading this book, go to your ads dashboard. The view that you should see is "all campaigns". At this time, ideally, you would have a single auto campaign for your book.

Ignore the graph and colored lines you see at the top. Scroll down to the chart of campaign data in columns. Make sure your columns have been customized and expanded.

1. Click on the auto campaign name.
2. Click on the ad group name.
3. You should see the campaign performance broken out by advertised ASIN. I like to see here how each of the formats are doing.

4. Next, focus on the specialized tabs that are on the left hand campaign navigation: Ads – Targeting – Negative targeting – search terms – ad group settings – history.
5. Click on targeting. You will see performance by the four targeting groups.
6. Compare performance of the targeting groups. Note the CTRs, CPC and conversion for each. For example, when looking at my auto campaign, I see that loose match and close match are the only targeting groups serving impressions. That's ok, especially with my new campaign. I note that loose match is getting 10x the impressions as close match with 2x the CTR and a CPC that's a few cents cheaper. Conversion is strong with ACOS 16% and 24%, respectively. How will those numbers change if I cut off the dead weight?
7. Click on search terms. Here you will see a list of all of the customer search terms that were matched to your targeting string, along with its performance metrics.
8. Sort by CTR, lowest to highest. Write down the terms with below .10% CTR that are not converting.
9. Click on negative targeting, then "add negative keywords". Add those non-converting low CTR search terms as negative exact match and hit save.
10. Return to search terms. Sort columns by Spend, highest to lowest. This view exposes the most egregious spenders; that is, the terms where you are spending a lot but not converting. If those terms have over 1000 impressions, copy them and add to negative targeting.
11. Next, sort by impressions, highest to lowest. Chances are the top impression terms that aren't converting have already been excluded by entering them into negative targeting. Continue to review the column, looking at the quality of targets that Amazon is matching you to. If you see an ASIN, check the ASIN to see if you think it's

a meaningful or relevant target. If not, add to your exclude list. Do same for the keywords.
12. Once you've reviewed your search terms, return to negative targeting. Add the keywords to the negative keywords but be sure that you click on "negative products" to add the ASINs you want to exclude.

You've now gotten rid of your top offenders and, by doing so, you should see CTR increase and ACOS decrease. You have effectively reallocated your budget (and the campaigns potential impressions) to focus on higher converting terms.

Recommendation: Continue to monitor this campaign, but don't make changes for at least one more week.

Basic Monitoring for Manual Ads

Monitoring Manual ads follows as similar process as with auto ads.

1. Click on the manual campaign name.
2. Click on the ad group name.
3. You should see the campaign performance broken out by advertised ASIN. Because I always include print and digital formats in my campaigns, I can see how each of the formats are performing.
4. Next, focus on the specialized tabs that are on the left hand campaign navigation: Ads – Targeting – Negative targeting – search terms – ad group settings – history.
5. Click on targeting. You will see performance by each of your individual targets. Review your targets and see where you can cut or dig your heels in.
6. Targets with impressions and no clicks. Do they have

over 1k impressions? If yes, pause it. If they are struggling to get impressions, review your bid against the suggestion. If you appear below range, increase your bid.
7. Targets with no impressions. Do you firmly believe these to be strong targets? If yes, review your bid. Where does your bid stand against the suggested range? Increase aggressively to see if you can kickstart impressions.
8. Targets with CTR <.10%. If you have at least 1k impressions, pause the target. This does not appear relevant because customers are not interested enough to click. Don't allow it to bring your overall campaign CTR down.
9. Click on Search Terms. Here you will see a list of all of the customer search terms that were matched to your targeting string, along with its performance metrics.
10. Sort by CTR, lowest to highest. Write down the terms with below .10% CTR that are not converting.
11. Click on negative targeting, then "add negative keywords" or "add negative products". Add those non-converting low CTR targets as negative exact match and hit save.
12. Return to search terms. Sort columns by Spend, highest to lowest. This view exposes the most egregious spenders; that is, the terms where you are spending a lot but not converting. If those terms have over 1000 impressions, copy them and add to negative targeting.
13. Next, sort by impressions, highest to lowest. Chances are the top impression terms that aren't converting have already been excluded by entering them into negative targeting. Continue to review the column, looking at the quality of targets that Amazon is matching you to. If you see an ASIN, check the ASIN to see if you think it's

a meaningful or relevant target. If not, add to your exclude list. Do same for the keywords.
14. Once you've reviewed your search terms, return to negative targeting. Add the keywords to the negative keywords but be sure that you click on "negative products" to add the ASINs you want to exclude.

CHAPTER 18
DEEP-DIVE MONITORING APPROACH

This deep-dive approach to ads improvement you want to take if you have a lot of campaigns and you need to clean things up, if you haven't done any optimization in a long time, or if you just want to get in deep to the reporting. It's meant to be an overall account "health check" to kick off optimization that you should be doing on a regular basis. Optimization is where many authors get stuck or lost in a data frenzy. There are so many features that it's hard to know what lever is the next one you should pull, so I've organized the optimization process into a checklist:

1. Analyze

2. Set your own benchmarks and performance

3. Find the sweet spot of what looks to be successful

4. Harvest targets

5. Double down on successes

6. Prioritize – choose a small number of campaigns and a small number of changes.

It doesn't matter which ad type you're monitoring; they all follow the basic principles. Go through this overall flow. Optimizing both your account and your campaigns is an investment. Staying objective while keeping your eye on the controllable inputs will improve your ads and go a long way in freeing up your time and headspace for writing.

Frequency / Cadence

I recommend monitoring your account a few times a week but limiting optimization to 2-3 times per month. You'll want to let changes sink in, and you'll need to be careful not to overcorrect. Any new campaigns should stay on at least one month. Keep an eye on new campaigns to ensure (a) that they take flight and (b) do not overspend.

Step 1: Analyze

Starting on your main dashboard, review campaigns across the board. Make observations without judgment. Note which campaigns may be outpacing others in impressions, CTR or conversions. To make this easier, I typically export the main dashboard (all columns). Run report the Search Term Report along with any others where you think you'll want to deep dive. Review the Search Term Report, sorting columns using the Basic Ads Monitoring approach. Make notes on your observations.

Tip: You don't need to run all of them every time you optimize.

Step 2: Set Benchmarks & Performance Targets

Use your own account, rather than another author's, to base performance targets. Here is where it's important not to compare yourself with other authors. Finding your own benchmarks helps you make your campaign monitoring focused on an objective.

Review the campaigns to understand where you are today and set performance targets. Keep it super simple; you don't need a performance target on everything. In fact, that's too messy and it probably won't work because it's not all directly actionable. Try focusing in on CTR to start since that's an indicator of relevance. For example, I have a handful of campaigns with varying CTR. I want to get them all over .15% to start. I'll pause keywords at .10 and below to start. I'll watch the impact for a week and then pause anything below .15%.

If I'm further along with inputs optimized, I'll set a target ACOS. To start, I may say everything needs to have less than 100% ACOS. Using ACOS for me is ok because I'm not in KU. This target is only a starter target but I will get more aggressive in weeks to come.

Don't stress on the math or strive for perfection. Your targets are not set in concrete – they can and should change over time. Take your baby steps towards where you want to go and set reasonable targets for yourself.

Tip: If you are in KU and still want something like an ACOS target, calculate a "revised" ACOS. You can do this by adding estimated royalties to the sales figured like this: ad spend / (sales+estimated KENP Royalties) = Revised ACOS.

Step 3: Finding the Sweet Spots

Based on your earlier analysis, try poking around your data to find some sweet spots. These "sweet spots" are areas of success. Ask yourself: Where do I see success? What's working? Can I replicate this success? Just remember that what works for one campaign may not apply to one with, say, a different targeting type. Did your head keyword match to long tail customer targets? Do you see a keyword theme? Of course, there may not even be sweet spots in every account or campaign.

Tip: I like to use Excel pivot tables excessively to find sweet spots. This lets me see trends a lot more quickly.

Step 4: Harvesting

Harvesting is simply gathering what you've planted in early campaign strategies. Your starting point should be your automatic keywords campaigns. Review the customer search terms that are matching to the different targeting groups. Note which targets are converting and put them into a manual campaign. Note which targets have high spend but are not converting; add them to your negative keywords. Doing this helps keep your relevance in check in the Amazon system.

Next, check your category campaigns. Review your search term report. See which ASIN pages your book is showing. If a matched ASIN is not converting, move it to negative targeting. If a matched ASIN is converting well, move it to a new ASIN or keyword campaign.

If there is one category that overall has weak performance, you can pause the target.

As I say with most of these steps, harvesting may not be appropriate for every campaign every single time you sit down to optimize. But keep this on your checklist to make sure you have it covered, if it's applicable.

Tip: Be diligent when pausing targets. Double check that the slider is on the "pause" state as the pause/enable slider sometimes reverts while you're still on the page. This is more likely to happen if you're moving quickly down the dashboard pausing many targets.

Step 5: Double Down

You're now an author-marketer now. That means your job is to find where Amazon is strongly responsive to your inputs and double down. This can mean:

• Adding more related targets to a keyword that is successful,

• Increasing your bids,

• Applying a riskier bid strategy, or

• Taking a successful ad and copying it using an entirely different targeting strategy. (If you have a great keyword campaign targeting comp authors, try a product targeted campaign with that author's ASINs.)

Step 6: Prioritize

Sometimes when monitoring campaigns, especially if you have many, you'll find that you have a long list of tweaks you can make. This may include new ad types, increasing bids, changing bid strategies, eliminating match types, or anything. Prioritize which campaigns you'll take action on and/or which changes you'll make. The risk of going all out and making too many changes is twofold: (1) you get confused and (2) if you need to roll back any changes your account may have a hard time recovering. So, take it slow. Keep it simple. Prioritization is your friend.

At some point, these steps will become second nature and you won't do them in order. You'll be nimble in applying campaign refinements.

Tip: Never de-prioritize turning off targets that are spending significantly and not converting. Trim the fat.

Optimizing Lockscreen Ads

Amazon doesn't share reporting by interest for Lockscreen ads, nor does it offer customized bidding. There are no levers to improving campaign performance.

Optimizing Your Bids

Even when your campaign appears healthy, stay on top of your bids. Monitor your bid against your CPC against the bid suggestions. Find areas where you can lower your bids and areas when you can spend more. Increase bids for targets with lower ACOS than your performance target Look at those with strong traffic volume. Look for those with room for higher impression share.

Tip: use your Search Impression Share Report to help inform your optimizing strategy.

Optimizing Sponsored Brands

You'll follow the same approach as the basic monitoring for performance metrics. But with Sponsored Brands, you have the ability to adjust your creative. How is your ad copy working? Is the landing page order or of the product images? While A/B split tests are not possible, you may want to experiment with a new ad.

Optimization on the Horizon

It looks like Amazon is going to roll out some automated optimization recommendations listed as "Opportunities" sometime in the coming months. It's already showing as a beta in some accounts, but it is currently only showing budget recommendations.

Recommendation: Set 30 day summary reports to run automatically each month. Monitor your campaigns twice per week and optimize weekly. Try to normalize the data and review performance for longer periods of time when making decisions. For example, I would look back 30 days to decide whether a target is non-converting; I don't want to cut out a solid keyword that just had a bad week! Kill off non-converting targets even if there is high CTR.

Tip: You don't need to look at every report every month. The point of automatic emails is so that you have the data once Amazon no longer retains it.

PART VI
LEVELING UP

"Scale" is a buzzword. It's a dangerous buzzword when coupled with inexperience. Scaling advertising means spending more to drive results. Authors are clamoring for guidance on how to scale. They're not alone; vendors and sellers are asking for same. I would say that it's the biggest challenge that advertisers face on the Amazon Ads platform. It's even harder in the books space because there are so many variables at both the nuanced book level and the ad campaign level, making it's difficult to directly replicate success. Pouring more money into your ads (increasing bids and/or budget) doesn't necessarily trigger conversions at the same rate. This can cause you to spend far more money on ads than is reasonable. Avoid this by getting in the right mindset before you tackle the tactics to level up your ads.

CHAPTER 19
MINDSET MATTERS

Any conversation about leveling up needs to address mindset, lest you get sucked into a frenzied vortex of advice. I find this to be one of the biggest problems for clients that come to see me, yet no one specifically comes to see me to change their mindset. I'm not a therapist. This is what comes out in conversation: they are disappointed in their ad performance but confused and anxious about ads in a way that hinders success.

Mindset Hot Spots and What to Do

You or someone you know are probably plagued with some of the red flags signaling that they're due for a mindset shift.

Impatience. You want to see sustained success quickly. Successful ads require experimentation, time to gather customer feedback. That is to say, enough impressions must serve on relevant targets that see strong CTR and conversions. Embrace experimentation. It's a key ingredient to success. But with that experimentation, financial and time investments are also required. It will take you 2 to 3 months in order to ramp up on Amazon Ads. And even at that point you are still going to continue experimenting, but you should at least have a few ideas about what is driving your success.

Comparisonitis triggers a sense of urgency. You're almost scrambling to catch up with others and the urgency is a false sense. Stop comparing yourself to others who are further along.

Wanting cheap clicks in spite of high budgets. Ads requires a level of continued financial investment to succeed. Being cheap about clicks but having a high budget is not a sustainable growth mindset. Keeping the bid down too low (for example, below $.20) will constrict your audience. While this tactic can be used for a long shot, long tail keyword, it's not sustainable across targets.

Emotional attachment to your project. Your project is complete, it's now time to step back, pull the personal out of the project and morph your business thinking into a product. I see this commonly play out with a refusal to change a poor quality cover.

Analysis paralysis. All the data points, data views and opinions can sometimes hinder your decision-making. The dashboard can easily cause decision overwhelm. You don't need to use every single feature to run solid ads. Start basic and prioritize what matters, remembering that: (1) *All data points are not actionable.* Focus on your controllable inputs. (2) *All metrics-related decisions are not created equal.* When you're stuck, consider whether the decision is a one-way door or a two-way door. With a one-way door, when you make that decision (and walk through the door), you're stuck. There's no way out. For example, you create an ambitious campaign with many targets. You are writing custom ad copy. That's a one-way door decision because you cannot delete the copy from your ad (once it's launched), nor can you edit it.

Consider what decisions are two-way doors. These are reversible. If you don't like what you see, you can walk right out. For example, you're on the fence about spending money on brand terms. If you have all of your brand terms collected on your master targeting list, you can easily try it out and pause it if you don't think it's providing value. That's a two-way door decision. No need to fret.

The complexity of ads is real. Amazon has not simplified its interface sufficiently for a very large swath of users (authors and others) and you are not alone.

CHAPTER 20
LEVELING UP TACTICS & STRATEGIES

Ads in general can help you scale your Amazon sales, but you need a baseline of organic sales to fuel ads. It's a virtuous cycle with organic sales feeding ads feeding organic sales, feeding ads, and so on.

If you have a few sales and a few clicks, you need growth. Growth is linear: you invest resources, your conversions increase. Many authors who come to me say they want to scale but the truth is they're not ready yet. Why not? They haven't yet found the gold (those keywords with high CTR that are converting) and trim the fat (remove targets that spend but do not convert) using basic optimization techniques. The methods to push growth are different than methods to truly scale.

Scaling ads means putting more money into ads to maintain positive return. Strategies to scale involve features or strategies that can be done without or with minimal extra effort. This is meant to be sustainable long term. Taking your ads to the next level is about both growth and scale

Bidding Approach: Fail Fast vs. Slow Dial

While many beginners are more comfortable with a Slow Dial approach, at some point you should hit a point where you pivot to Fail Fast. This path includes bidding to express the most you're willing to pay for a click. This number would be based on your series read through value.

Bidding Tactic: Bidding to Value

If you are a series writer, hopefully by now you have calculated your series read through value (RTV). In classic marketing speak, this is your lifetime value, or the value of a click on an ad for book one of your series. If you know that you have X% series read through and the RTV is $8 book, use that to calculate how high you can bid on some targets. By "some targets," I'm referring to an elite set of golden targets that are known converters. I'm not encouraging you to go as high as $8 if that's your RTV, but you should be using that rather than just the return on book one alone to evaluate a target's willingness to spend.

To figure out bidding to value for a single book that is not part of a series, you can take the book's and work out the value like this:

	format	price	royalty		% of revenue			
					20%	30%	40%	50%
Book A	print		9.99	3.27	$0.65	$0.98	$1.31	$1.64
	ebook		5.99	2.1	$0.42	$0.63	$0.84	$1.05
					$0.00	$0.00	$0.00	$0.00
Book B	print		9.99	3.06	$0.61	$0.92	$1.22	$1.53
	ebook		5.99	2.1	$0.42	$0.63	$0.84	$1.05
Book C	print	N/A						
	ebook		4.99	3.45	$0.69	$1.04	$1.38	$1.73

Bidding to Value: create your own bid ranges based on royalties

In this example, I'm trying to see what my bid ranges should be for these books. I see that I get the most value ($3.45) from Book C. I want to create my own bid ranges based on percentages of that value. I have some golden targets for which I want to bid very aggressively. I won't go up to $3.45, but what if I am willing go to 50% of my royalty and bid $1.73? I'm going to set that as my stretch bid. Most other targets, I want to get down to closer to 20% ($.69) for a medium performing keyword, but for some I'm sure I'll be willing to go to 30-40%. This exercise gives me my own bid ranges which are customized to my own pricing and royalty structure.

Tip: You can also use this exercise if you have as series but not sure you have the right read through data yet.

Targeting: Next Generation Ads

When you build your initial targeting list, you had core targets such as Also Boughts. These change over time. Make sure that you're updating your segments and expanding those segments with a new generation of related targets by scraping a layer deeper. For example, you started with 5 strong authors who were appearing in your Also Boughts. Now go to author 1, author 2, author 3, author 4 and author 5, and then scrape each of their Also Boughts.

Recommendation: Do this for your comps and Also Boughts, at minimum. When creating ads for them, be sure to separate out each author's Also Boughts into separate ad groups.

Targeting: Long Tail targeting

Long tail targeting is similar to the next generation ads, only you're expanding on key words that are working. Expand your key terms to get more specific. Traffic is expected to be lower due to lower demand, but the specificity should drive a higher value customer who is more likely to convert. You can get more specific by using the suggestions in the Amazon campaign builder, or you can farm from your ad's search term report.

Recommendation: Do this for your top 3 keywords, at minimum. When creating ads for them, be sure to separate out each of them into individual ad groups or campaigns. For example, if you are advertising a romantic suspense book, you would put romance keywords in one ad group (or even campaign and suspense related keywords in another.

Targeting: Micro targeting

Sometimes, try as you might, you just cannot increase the volume of impressions on a strong converting target. In these cases, consider micro-targeting. Create a campaign with a very tight circle of targets. Doing this forces a dedicated spend to these targets and gives great insight into the opportunity. I recommend keeping the circle very small. Here's an example: If you are targeting J.D. Robb in a campaign, along with a list of other authors. You see that the phrase J.D. Robb has a high CTR that converts very well to sales but you can't seem to get the ad to show more. Create a microtargeted campaign with J.D. Robb only. You can use just that one term, or you can take less than 5 high converting relevant terms and add those as well. Keep the targeting microscopic.

Targeting: Branded Targets and Brand Defense Ads

A branded target is your own author name, series, book title or ASIN. Branded targets should always be included on your master targeting list. They are often the cheapest clicks you can get due to high relevance. You may see in an automatic targeting campaign that the top term receiving clicks is your author name or other branded term.

It's inevitable that you'll ask, "Why pay for clicks that would otherwise come to me organically?" It's a smart question for every author to consider and consciously address one way or the other.

If you are against advertising against your own brand targets, use the master list as negative targets in all of your auto campaigns. This excludes the terms from your campaign. You'll have to negate them at the campaign level in every new auto campaign.

While it may seem wasteful to bid on your own name thinking the customer was obviously looking for you and your books, remember that people are easily distracted. An intriguing ad by a competitor could steal the sale from a shopper searching for you by name – this is someone who has the HIGHEST probability of converting to a sale. This is worth protecting.

You can run brand defense ads in a way that protects your market share, positioning and mind share against a competitor. You're attempting to safeguard your brand by closing any opening that could allow a competitor to slip in and take a customer. Here's an example: A new author comes online and starts targeting a bestselling author. The bestselling author's customers are trickling away – whether or not they realize it at first. The bestselling author then starts running ads targeting himself. This closes the gap blocking the new author from grabbing the bestselling author's customers.

As in the previous example, this is primarily used if you are a well-known author in your genre or sub-genre and have a popular series or book. Due to your rank or status, competing authors may bid high on queries containing your terms in hopes of attracting readers.

If you want to take this approach, build your branded target list by including all variations of your author name, book titles, ASINs, series names. Determine where you want to defend the search experience or on book detail pages. If you want search, you'll want to consider sponsored brands, or sponsored products keyword search. If covering your own detail pages are important, you'll want to do Sponsored Product ASIN campaigns targeting those ASINs.

Although ultimately you should be paying a low CPC, you should determine how high to bid: Do you want to aggressively defend? If not, then bid low hoping that relevance can drive low cost protection.

Recommendation: Considering using brand defense for the following scenarios:(1) As brand defense. Buy the space so someone else can't. (2) For brand building. You've creating more exposure to your books. (3) For psychological reasons. If targeting your own detail pages, you give readers reinforcement of the purchase they're about to make.

Targeting: Use Broad Match Modifiers

Broad match modifiers are keywords that have a '+' in front of the keyword. They can be used when you want to go broad with a small degree of specificity. For example, if you use the "+paranormal romance books". To match with this target, the customer search term must contain "paranormal." This could match to "paranormal romance novels" but not "romance books".

Targeting: Poaching Pre-Orders

Poaching pre-orders is fun for a new release, or your own pre-order, if your pre-order is coming out sooner than the target. Your book should be a juicy offering and you can entice readers who are browsing pre-orders to choose your book and be able to read it now.

You can find pre-orders by going to the Kindle Store. On the top navigation bar (below the search bar), there is an "Advanced Search" button. This allows you to search for kindle books by keywords, author, title, publisher, on various subjects, by language, or by publication date. In order to see which pre-orders are coming out in the next month or two, you would search by publication date in a date range after the current month and year.

While customers may still pre-order the book on the detail page, targeting preorders may drive purchases of your book by customers who are looking to read NOW.

Targeting: Index on the purchase path

Indexing on the purchase path is considered an advanced tactic worth investing in if you are already exhausting other growth levers. The challenge here is that it's difficult to employ in the books category but considered an advanced strategy for non-books on Amazon.

Fifty-one percent of global surveyed book buyers are undecided on a title to buy when they start shopping, according to a recent Kantar study.[1] Sixty percent of book buyers research online before purchasing[2] That's a lot of searches, and a lot of potential paths to purchase.

The goal here is to insert yourself on the purchase path for new customers. When customers come into the Amazon ecosystem, they start with a search in the search bar. They may have started under all product search in the drop-down menu, or they may have started their search within the books category. Regardless of where the query begins, Amazon will deliver search results. These search results pull the user into a web of options that they will now be combing through.

If the query began as an "all product search", the user may then click on a subcategory like Kindle Store or Books, or even deeper into sub-genre options to further filter search results. Amazon does not want users to have to perform *another* search. Instead, they want the search results to be valuable enough that the consumer has an array of solid options. Remember, Amazon does not just want a customer to buy one book or one widget or one whatever product within a shopping session; Amazon wants users to find multiple things that they like in order to increase the order value.

This is part of the reason why ads work like recommendations for shoppers browsing. Consider the purchase path of the user who has done a single query and been thrown into a sea of books. What happens next? They scroll through the search results. These may include both organic results and they may include paid. It doesn't matter. The user is scrolling until they find a book that they like. This is likely to happen on page one and probably less so on page two even less likely, and the further down the results pages. Let's imagine now that the user still hasn't seen your book, even though it should be an important keyword for your book. The user is on a book's detail page. Where are you?

It's very important that you show up for the terms you want to show up for. For instance, if my book is an RPG fantasy, and I don't show up on one or two pages of the search results, I ask myself why not? It's in my meta-data. How can you make a stronger connection? You're probably already advertising against a term like RPG Fantasy, but you can do more. Ask yourself who does index against it? In other words, when you type in "RPG fantasy," which books show? Get on the detail pages for those books that are showing for your most valuable keywords.

Inserting yourself on the purchase path for the high value search terms is intended to do two things: of course drive incremental ad sales and organic sales. Clearly, you're looking for incremental sales by serving an ad. But, if done at scale, the hope is that it improves your connectedness – or relevance – to that keyword and improves your organic visibility against that keyword.

This is a slow game requiring aggressive bids against those high value purchase path targets. The very long-term thinking here is that initially the search terms may be expensive. As your relevance increases and conversions are healthy, your CPC may in fact come down because of your newly found relevance. This is an approach that is designed to improve your sales velocity and your own flywheel on Amazon. Remember, when you improve organic sales, you are more likely to improve your advertising return as well. They each feed the virtual cycle that lifts both.

Recommendation: Inserting yourself on the purchase path is only for patient, professional authors who have meticulously curated their product packaging and who have a strong understanding on their classification and their comps.

Strategy: Integrating with Other Marketing Efforts

Ads do not operate in a silo. One of the best things that you can do to lift your Amazon ads is to integrate with your other marketing efforts. Although a very frugal or new advertiser could say, "I'm doing a Bookbub deal so I'm going to turn off

Amazon ads", a more savvy advertiser will say, "I'm doing a Bookbub deal so I'm *actually going to increase* my Amazon ad spend." Amazon ads work better when there is more traffic coming to your detail page. Integrating your marketing plan and stacking ads and promotions is the best thing you can do for your ads. Don't be binary about the channels that you used to drive sales on Amazon. Any activity, including driving inbound traffic, improves Amazon's data on your book and will be reflected in new Also Boughts and relevance.

Strategy: International Expansion

Ads for KDP authors are available in the United States, Canada, United Kingdom, Germany, France, Italy, Spain and Australia. If your book is in English, consider expanding to English-language marketplaces first. The browse trees are owned by local country teams, so they are crafted differently. User browse patterns are also different by country. With this in mind, your ads may perform differently even though the underlying ad mechanics function uniformly across marketplaces.

Start with basic automatic and category ads in any new country. This will give you an idea of how your book connects to the local catalog. Use trends in your auto campaigns to start crafting a localized targeting approach

PART VII
TIPS, TRICKS & TROUBLE

It's inevitable that you're going to need to troubleshoot your ads. Use this section as your reference guide.

CHAPTER 21
TIPS TO LIVE BY

1. Start off organized with good account hygiene. Create portfolios and use forward-thinking naming conventions. Schedule reports to run monthly.
2. Keep targeting tight, striving for quality over quantity. Avoid keyword targeting duplication on the same ASIN.
3. Bid to win. Consider a Fail Fast approach over the Slow Dial approach. Rip the Band-Aid off!
4. Spend Control. Don't start a campaign with under a $10 daily budget. Control your monthly ad costs leveraging Portfolio budgets.
5. Negative targeting is Optimization's best friend. Exploit it to keep frivolous click spend at bay.
6. Use tactics wisely. Don't just jump to use every feature because it exists. Using more features doesn't help you run better ads. Keep ads simple using only basic features until you nail targets. Avoid custom text and bid modifiers until you know what works.
7. Have patience throughout your learning process. You don't need to lose your mind learning ads. Experiment and learn.

8. Start in the US but don't ignore other English-speaking countries

CHAPTER 22
TROUBLESHOOTING

The Sponsored Ads program was designed to meet the needs of all kinds of product lines: shoes, watches, headphones, blenders. It was intentionally agnostic because the more generic (or generally applicable) a feature is, the faster it can scale to more users. Since opening Sponsored Ads to books, they've come to learn that it's hard to make generic work for books and other media.

This means that not all ad options or features work effectively for books. And sometimes, when the support team or marketing email says, "It is available for book advertisers," it does not necessarily mean it really *works*. To make matters worse, help content or advice from customer service agents is often misguided about book advertising. Still, there is a lot of great information published by Amazon about its ad products; you just need to know what to filter out (see the Tools & Resources chapter for more).

Every advertiser needs to troubleshoot at some point. There is a learning curve and there are growing pains on any PPC platform. Some challenges just arise, and you need to adjust your strategy or modify your tactics. This is not to say that you did something wrong. It's standard practice to run ads for a while, get some performance data back and then tweak the ads accordingly. So, while I label this section "troubleshooting," it's not *trouble* in the way of a printer jam. You can't simply skip some of these things that are just a part of the standard operating procedure for learning ads.

On top of that, Amazon is slow at fixing the issues that block author success. Why is this so? Amazon's Sponsored Ads program was designed to meet the needs of all kinds of product lines, so it was intentionally agnostic to make it easier and faster to scale to more users. Since opening Sponsored Ads to books in 2015, they've come to learn that it's hard to make the generic work for books.

Ad Rejections

"My ad was rejected. What next?"

It's inevitable that at some point you will have an ad rejected. These are the main reasons:

1. Your cover or content is inappropriate. If the cover is inappropriate, assess whether it makes sense to modify it to meet the guidelines. If it's your content (like glorifying drugs), you're out of luck.
2. Your cover is inappropriate and you believe Amazon is wrong. Before you get rooted in your belief, go back and read the Guidelines. This issue is very common in the Romance category. Readers like covers with sexy images. But Amazon has strict rules about how much skin can show and what the image may suggest. Read the Guidelines closely.
3. Amazon moderators have identified a typo, or grammar or content issue with your custom ad copy. Once

rejected, the ad should appear in your drafts tab. At this point, you'll need to copy the campaign to a new one and make the edit on the custom text. Then you will need to re-submit the ad. This is not convenient, but custom text is a unique feature that is not standard across advertiser types so it is not yet editable.

Campaign is rejected during moderation

"My campaign was rejected but why?"

First, check your email – the notification should include a reason. Sometimes it's because the campaign was vague, or you're not clear about how it's related to your book. If it's unclear or ambiguous, go back to Book Ads Policy. If you ultimately disagree with the decision, you can appeal it. To do this, open your ads account and go to the support center. Choose the ad type that you're having the issue with, then choose "campaign rejected."

It may take some back and forth for you to finally get an answer. It's ok to keep appealing.

Note that "someone else is doing it" is not a sufficient appeal.

Received Rejection Email but Campaign Delivering

"I got an email that my campaign was rejected but the dashboard says my campaign is delivering. Was this an error?"

The status that you see is a campaign level status, which is accurate but misleading. The ads are technically moderated at the ad level so you need to drill down to see the status of the ad group. Double click on the ad group to see the moderation status.

Inconsistent Moderation

"My Romance cover was rejected but I see steamier covers live on the site. Why?"

This is frustrating for authors. Sometimes there can be a slight nuance in the cover that makes it through the moderation process. Other times, it's a human error. The reviewer believes it's ok, when it's not.

Lockscreen Ad Rejected

Due to the sensitive nature of the prominent placement on the Kindle device, Lockscreen Ads are subject to stricter guidelines. Some content that can be advertised using other ad types is not eligible for Lockscreen Ads. Read the Guidelines thoroughly for the additional rules on Lockscreen.

No Impressions

"Why is my campaign getting zero impressions?"

If you consider the metrics waterfall, you know that impressions are an input metric having multiple levers to dial up or dial down. Your target needs to be relevant and your bids need to be high enough. Alternatively, your ad could be suspended and you don't realize it. Be sure to double check your ad status at the ad group level (double click on campaign, then double click on each ad group).

Low Impressions

"Why is my campaign getting very low impressions?"

Assuming that you're relevant enough to get any impressions, focus on your bid. Is your bid high enough? Evaluate this by comparing your bid to the CPC. Is your CPC coming in at the same level as your bid? If so, you may need to increase the bid. Before doing so, compare your CPC with the suggested bid range. You can often use this as a gauge to validate an increase.

Impressions but no clicks

"I have impressions but no clicks."

A low CTR signals that customers are not interested in your book within the context of where your ad was shown. Re-assess your targets. Are you targets really the right company for your book?

Clicks but No Conversions

"I'm getting clicks but no sales or pages read."

My first question is, "How many clicks are you getting?" If the sample size is too small, this is not statistically significant. If you have over 1k impressions, evaluate your detail page. Are you meeting the expectations you set when advertising against a particular target?

Few Targets Working

"I have X targets but only Y are getting any impressions."

Are you bidding enough? It's possible that you need to be more competitive than on some targets.

Are you targets popular? If you are using obscure keywords or ASINs, it's very possible that the reach opportunity is quite limited.

How many targets do you have? It's possible that this is the lazy Algorithm. Have you ever seen a campaign that consistently pushes all targets in a campaign? No? Me, neither. It would be great if Amazon would publish some author data on this.

Keyword Volume

"Everyone says I need 100 or 300 or 1000 keywords."

Quality over quantity should be your mantra. Keep your keyword volume lower than the large suggestions, and keep it closely aligned with your book. Many times, authors reference the 1000 keyword limit in a campaign but this is a technical limit; this is not a recommendation.

Not Consuming Budget

"Amazon won't take my money."

It's a well-known secret that Amazon's superpower is leaving KDP author cash on the table. If you've already aggressively increased bids and can't get your ad dollars spent, try microtargeting.

Maxxing Out Budget

"Amazon keeps telling me I need to increase my budget from $X to $Y. What should I do?"

A recent increase in budget notifications urge authors via email, notifications, dashboard tips to increase their budgets. The new budget reporting shares insight into how much you're within budget (and delivering ads) vs what you missed out on.

Recommendation: Sometimes notifications are based on stale data. Other times, we see that the conversation does not maintain a steady enough state to warrant increasing. Take these new suggestions with care. If you do increase your budget, closely monitor CVR. If you are not converting at the same rate, you need to determine whether the budget increase makes sense or whether you moved out of your sweet spot. I rarely take a budget recommendation unless my ACOS (or revised ACOS) is sufficiently low.

Dashboard Clutter

"I've created so many ads that now I'm afraid to clean it up."

Clients who come to me for cleanup are usually coming from a sprint challenge where they are told to keep creating ads. Don't create too many ads unless you have a very clear strategy on how to do it in a way that makes sense for your goals.

Recommendation: Focus first on housekeeping. (1) Create portfolios, (2) Rename campaigns to allow you to view key campaign features more easily, (3) Run reports to understand what's working and what's not, (4) remove duplication (re-using targets across campaigns for the same ASIN), (5) aim to reduce your campaigns.

Campaign Volume

"I was told I have to create at least 10 campaigns per book."

I'm really not sure who made up this number. It's simply not backed by data. Sure, many authors have had success running multiple ads for a single book, but 10 is not warranted. This is especially true with newer features such as ad groups. Leveraging ad groups to build a logical campaign structure can reduce the number of campaigns you need to put out there for visibility. Features like bidding strategy and match targeting also drive efficiency.

What's Working?!

"I can't tell what's working."

See messy dashboard.

Costly Clicks (spending too much)

"My ads are too expensive"

These are the things that cost authors unwarranted cash:

1. Bidding too low while using a high bid modifier. You are "only bidding" $.50 but you've used placement bidding to increase by x% or you're using dynamic

bidding up and down. Remove bid modifiers and make sure your campaign bidding strategy is either "fixed bids" or "down only".
2. Bidding high on Top of Search before nailing your targets.
3. Trying to scale up the campaign before driving spend efficiency.
4. Using dynamic up and down bidding before you're ready. See number one above.
5. Using dynamic up and down when most of your conversions are pages read. This is not a signal for dynamic bidding.

Ads Stopped Working

"My ads were working fine for about a month and then dropped off a cliff... the algorithm changed!"

When I see these claims of a change, there hasn't usually been a meaningful change in ads. A number of times when this was claimed, we worked with engineers to deep dive, and found nothing unusual —"working as designed" (it's the dreaded response of any technical support ticket).

Instead of blaming the algorithm, think of the many other factors that could change your individual ad performance, such as reader behavior or auction competition. Don't underestimate signals that you may need some optimization.

Auto Ads Only showing for self or general terms

"Auto Ads are showing only for self or general terms – why?"

This is often due to a "cold start." A cold start is a brand-new author who throws a book on Amazon that isn't really getting any sales, so they have no data to feed the Amazon ads algorithm. If you are a cold start, you may not quite be ready to start advertising. I encourage you to work on marketing efforts to drive traffic to your Amazon detail page.

Recommendation: Audit your metadata in the KDP portal and confirm it's on point. If you don't want to spend on your own terms, negate your brand terms to push Amazon to come up with more. Keep ads running but invest in efforts to push traffic to your book's Amazon detail page.

Problems with Lockscreen Ads

Because Kindle devices are semi-connected, the campaign is likely to under-report your sales and pages read attributed. Also, if the ad is spending well, there are limited ways to optimize. This means ads can appear to get expensive. More commonly is the issue that the ads do not take flight. Lockscreen Ads for KDP authors is essentially a remnant ad product, falling in priority behind the premium ads from big spenders (books and non-books) who have placed expensive campaigns with guaranteed impressions.

It's important to understand that readers engaging with Lockscreen are potentially in a different place in your sales funnel. They may not be opening the device to shop (they can on the tablet but not on the eReader). If they are on the device to engage other than shop, your ad needs to be even more powerful.

Print Edition not in ASIN picker

"When I go to create an ad, I don't see my print edition."

If your print edition is being listed via KDP, it should appear in the ASIN picker. If it doesn't, contact Amazon Ads. If your print edition is being published through Ingram, it is not eligible to be advertised on Amazon.

CHAPTER 23
TOOLS & RESOURCES

You're not alone. There are many resources out there to support your ads endeavor. Some paid, some are free.

Contacting Amazon Ads Support

Ads specialists are often not fully trained on author and/or book nuances. When contacting Amazon Ads support, aim to use the right terms to help accelerate getting your problem addressed. Many times things are not fixed because the wrong language is used or there is a rambling note that needs to be unpacked and deciphered.

I have yet to get a meaningful response from any of the tickets I've opened. I don't know why I do it anymore… Actually, this little flashback is why I do it.

> employee: There's a big problem with X.
>
> manager: Show me the contacts.
>
> employee: There aren't any contacts.
>
> manager: We can't prioritize this.

This means one of two things: (1) that truly authors are not contacting Amazon about important issues (I know, I know, sometimes it's easier just to post in a FB group); or (2) authors HAVE contacted but the email is so long and convoluted that it ends up getting misclassified and the crux of the matter gets missed.

Authors, stick to the point. This is not the time for an essay or a personal diatribe or rant. You can always do that later (or if it escalates). Stick to one issue at hand; mixing up 10 things into one will delay a response or an actual fix. Use the correct terminology (use this book as a reference). When submitting a contact, use this framework:

Problem:

ASIN / Campaign ID:

Background:

What happened: [be succinct]

What [you believe] should have happened:

Please investigate and advise.

Thank you,

[insert name]

Recommendation: Help address advertising concerns by make sure Amazon knows it's an issue for authors. Contact them, regardless of whether you think it will get fixed. Create separate tickets for separate issues.

Amazon Ads Help Content: advertising.amazon.com

Don't underestimate the educational resource directly in the ads console. For basic questions about metrics definitions, it's a better resource than any Facebook group (where I see wrong answers posted by well-intentioned folks). This is particularly true for questions around attribution. It should be your first stop in trying to understand anything. Just remember to read the help content and note if there is a specific KDP callout.

Third Party Tools

From time to time, you'll find that third party (i.e., non-Amazon) tools may help you get on the road to ads success. These include:

Keyword Search tools

Helium10

KDPSpy

Merchant Words

Publisher Rocket

Data scrapers

AMZScout

PickASIN

ScrapeHero

GLOSSARY

Above the fold (ATF): Ads that show above the "scroll line" so readers may see the ad before scrolling further on the site. Most ads that appear in desktop search are ATF. Placements on the detail page are a mix of ATF and below the fold.

Ad creative: The elements that display to a customer, including book cover, price, star rating, and custom elements, if any.

Ad groups: These are like folders within a campaign and are used to manage and organize your ads. You may organize by theme or targeting strategy.

Ad slot or **ad widget**: These terms are used interchangeably and refer to a specific ad placement.

Ad type: This refers to the ad product within Sponsored Ads, of which there are three currently available to KDP Authors: Sponsored Products, Sponsored Brands and Lockscreen Ads.

Ad: This is your bundle (book, ad creative, bid, targeting strategy) that gets sent to auction and then shown to the customer.

Advantage Central: The retail portal for the Advantage program.

Glossary

Advantage: The retail program allowing vendors to sell physical media products on consignment.

Advertising cost of sale (ACOS): The percentage of sales you made from your ad spend. This is calculated by dividing total ad spend by total sales from advertising. This does not account for any sales of print-on-demand books from non-Amazon services (such as IngramSpark) and does not consider pages read for books in Kindle Unlimited.

Also-boughts: The widget on the detail page that shows what other customers bought in addition to the book featured on that detail page. this widget disappears from time to time as Amazon does detail page testing.

Amazon Ads: The advertising program at Amazon that offers different ad types to different types of entities including endemic (seller, vendor, KDP author) and non-endemic (those who do not have products listed for sale on Amazon).

Attribution: This refers to your sales attribution, or the total value of books sold as a result of the click on your ad. Attribution methodology will depend on which ad type you're using and, at this time, does not include Kindle Unlimited metrics.

Auction: The mechanism that brings together a group of ads and selects which ads will appear on the page for a reader and how much you will pay for that reader's click.

Audience: The group of people in your target. For example, the group that would use the keyword you have selected or the view the page that you have targeted in your ad.

Average Cost Per Click (ACPC): The average cost you actually pay based on your expressed bid.

Glossary

Below the fold (BTF): Any ad that is placed on site where the user needs to scroll to view the ad. Many Sponsored Products that appear on the detail page are BTF.

Beta: A test version of a feature or ad-type product before it releases broadly. Based on the test learnings, the feature may never fully make it to market. Sometimes it remains available to a limited audience and sometimes it is removed completely.

Bid strategy: A control for your bids that you set which determines whether you want Amazon to adjust your bid at auction in accordance with its forecasting.

Bid: The highest amount that you are willing to pay for a click on your ad. Very often your ACPC will be below your expressed bid.

Brand competitive set (also known as Comps): A marketing term used to identify the principal group of competitors for a company. Competitive sets in Sponsored Ads are typically used to help develop targeting strategies.

Brand halo: This is a concept used in Amazon's sales attribution where total sales and units sold may reflect any product in your catalog, not solely the advertised book. This means that your sales attribution may include a purchase of any product in your catalog after the customer clicked on your advertised ASIN. This methodology depends on which ad type you're using. In July of 2020, Amazon removed this halo from Sponsored Products for KDP authors and will only report on the advertised ASIN.

Budget consumption: The ratio of ad spend to budget expressed. It is quite common for book ads to have a low consumption ratio, making it difficult to effect and estimate ad scaling.

Budget: The maximum amount you are willing to spend on a campaign or group of campaigns in a portfolio for a selected time period.

Campaign audit: A review of your campaign(s) to identify areas of improvement and optimization.

Campaign: In traditional marketing, a campaign is a series of ad messages that share a single idea and theme. In digital advertising, a campaign will refer to a set of ads (or ad groups).

Carousel or **Carousel ads**: This is typically referencing the Sponsored Products horizontal ad slot on the product detail page, where the user can scroll through pages of ads.

Click through rate (CTR): The percentage of ad impressions that were clicked on compared to the entire number of clicks [CTR(%) = (clicks ÷ impressions) × 100].

Conversion rate (CVR): The percentage of users who click "buy" compared to all users who clicked on the ad.

Cost-per-click (CPC): The cost of one click on your ad. See also, Average cost-per-click.

Creative: *See* ad creative

Detail page: Your book description page on Amazon. Also known as sales page or listing page.

Flight: A term borrowed from television advertising that means the timing around when a commercial will air. In digital ads, this is often used to refer to the duration of an ad campaign.

Impression: Your ad being displayed to a customer. This does not mean that they actually saw it.

Interstitial page: This is sometimes called a "between-the-page". An interstitial page may appear on the Lockscreen Ads flow if the reader clicks on an ad when not connected to the internet.

Keyword targeting: Targeting content that contains specific keywords or phrases.

Keyword: Specific word(s) entered into a search function that results in a list of products related to the keyword.

Kindle Direct Publishing Select (KDPS): Sometimes referred to as "Select". Enrolling a book in KDPS puts your book into the Kindle Unlimited subscription program for readers (See below). You earn royalties on pages read and are bound to exclusivity on Amazon.

Kindle Unlimited (KU): Kindle Unlimited is a subscription program for readers that allows them to read as many books as they want for a single monthly fee.

Listing page: Your book description page on Amazon. Also known as sales page or detail page.

Lockscreen Ads: An ad type within Sponsored Ads that is exclusive to KDP authors and book publishers. The ads appear on Kindle devices. Note that, while Lockscreen is available as a self service ad product for book advertisers, it is not an exclusive placement. There is another managed ads premium service that takes priority for this inventory.

Managed ads: A display-ads program within Sponsored Ads that has a large minimum buy-in. Advertisers have an assigned account manager and a campaign manager who sets up the ads.

Metadata: The back-end data that provides information about your book to retail and advertising systems.

Negative keyword: A keyword target that you designate to exclude from your targeting.

Pay per click (PPC): An advertising pricing model in which advertisers pay only based on how many users clicked on an ad.

Performance metrics: The measurement of digital ad campaigns with action-based goals such as impressions, click-throughs, or sales.

Placement: The location of the ad. Also called an ad slot or ad widget.

Portfolio: A "folder" method used to organize campaigns based on a theme, as defined by the advertiser. You may also manage your ad budget at the Portfolio level.

Reach: How much of an audience sees an ad. For Sponsored Ads, we usually consider this to be the number of impressions.

Read-through or Read-through value (RTV): A calculation used to determine how many readers enter a series at book 1 and continue on to consume books 2, 3, and beyond.

Relevance: A term that refers to how meaningful ad systems deem your ad to be to customers.

Return on ad spend (ROAS): A metric used by advertisers to measure how much revenue they earned that can be attributed to the expense of an ad campaign.

Revised ACOS: For titles enrolled in KDP Select, ACOS is not a sufficient gauge of ad evaluation. A revised ACOS includes royalties on pages read. This is calculated by adding sales plus royalties. This is total income. Then divide ad spend by total income.

Sales page: Your book description page on Amazon. Also known as listing page or detail page.

Seasonality: A characteristic of a time series in which the data experiences regular and predictable changes, which recur every calendar year.

Self-service ads: The Sponsored Ads program that is available via login to Advertising.amazon.com. Users are expected to use the help content to address issues; there is a "contact us" form for advanced troubleshooting.

Sellers: Third party resellers who use Seller Central to manage their product listings on Amazon.

Share of voice (SOV): The percentage of ad space on a page that is filled by a single brand; for example, if only one brand has ads appearing on a page, then that brand has 100% SOV.

Sponsored Ads: The set of self-service ad types available via Amazon Advertising.

Sponsored Brands: A Sponsored Ads ad type that allows advertisers to feature three books in a single "headline" ad slot and drive users to a custom landing environment.

Sponsored Display: A Sponsored Ads ad type that enables advertisers to run simple display ads in a self-service manner without requiring a large minimum spend.

Sponsored Products: The longest running Sponsored Ads ad type that allows advertisers to bid on targets and promote ASINs to customers in search and on detail pages.

Targeted advertisement: An ad that is shown only to users exhibiting specific attributes or in a specific context.

Targeting: The mechanism that allows you to reach a certain set of readers.

CONGRATULATIONS!

You're on your way to more successful ads. In the meantime...

Let's Keep in Touch

Sign up for news and updates to this book here:

www.bookgeeksmarketing.com/amazon-ad-book-news-and-updates

If you have feedback or questions about content, drop a line to:

info@bookgeeksmarketing.com

For 1:1 consultation, contact me here:

https://www.bookgeeksmarketing.com/services-4

If you'd like a step-by-step self-paced class, I teach the Amazon Ads course in Mark Dawson's Self Publishing Formula Ads for Authors.

ACKNOWLEDGMENTS

This was a bigger feat than I expected. I couldn't have done it without a great team! Research assistants Lydia Montgomery and Johnny Lindell kickstarted the project early on. Micki Margot and Amy Luning came in and helped me cross the finish line this summer with re-reads galore. You ladies are amazing!

A big shout outs to:

Sam Trammel for the extraordinarily generous editorial guidance that was probably a premature review

Beta readers Deborah, Susan, and Johnny

Mark Dawson for inspiring me to write a non-fiction book and for sharing his process.

SPF Community and 20Booksto50k Facebook groups for teaching me how to self-publish throughout the last few years

Colleen Aubrey for stopping me on the street near Amazon's Wainwright building to talk about ads for KDP authors, and for the opportunity to work in a space that I'm wildly passionate about

And

Samantha Margot, my daughter/sometimes editor, who knows more about Amazon Ads than any normal kid should.

Thank you all!

Made in the USA
Coppell, TX
26 July 2022

80477422R00092